René Magritte

Titles in the series Critical Lives present the work of leading cultural figures of the modern period. Each book explores the life of the artist, writer, philosopher or architect in question and relates it to their major works.

In the same series

René Magritte

Patricia Allmer

REAKTION BOOKS

For Zoë

Published by
Reaktion Books Ltd
Unit 32, Waterside
44–48 Wharf Road
London N1 7UX, UK
www.reaktionbooks.co.uk

First published 2019
Copyright © Patricia Allmer 2019

Printed and bound in Great Britain by Bell & Bain, Glasgow

A catalogue record for this book is available from the British Library

ISBN 978 1 78914 151 1

Contents

Duane Michals, *Magritte with Hand Over Face Exposing One Eye*, 1965, gelatin silver print.

Introduction: 'Meet me at the carousel!'

The show is beginning! It has begun!
Pierre Souvestre and Marcel Allain, *Juve contre Fantômas* (1911)[1]

Interviewer: 'Tell us your life story in ten lines at most.'
Magritte: 'Ten lines is far too much for me.'
Magritte, 1967[2]

As I write, a new Twitter notification shows a photograph of a protest poster being held aloft. The backdrop is familiar – skyscrapers, blue sky and the word 'New' of the New York Public Library are visible – while the poster features an image reworking René Magritte's famous painting of a pipe that is not a pipe. Instead of the pipe's bowl we see the grinning face of the current American president, Donald Trump, while Magritte's familiar line 'Ceci n'est pas une pipe', asserting the difference between representation and reality, is rewritten in the poster as 'Ceci n'est pas un président' (with a final mocking negation of Trump, 'UNPRESIDENT', written underneath). The poster presents an act of Situationist *détournement*, ripping the image from its familiar context (the gallery, the coffee-table art book) and thrusting it into a new one (political protest) to exploit its potential to generate urgent new significance. This détourned Magritte image, generated by the Occupy Design UK Graphics Archive, now appears on numerous commercial items, from bumper stickers and T-shirts to babygrows and coffee cups.

Few artists have had their work cited, imitated, appropriated or détourned as often as Magritte; few artists have created a visual vocabulary, a lexicon of images of supreme ambiguity and supple indetermination, which can be appropriated to express wildly different situations. What works for Rihanna's limited run of ten 'Ceci n'est pas un Delvaux' bags, retailing exclusively at Barneys in 2014 at $7,350, also works to express political protest. And what works for the protest poster also works for its opposite, as is clear from the cover of Charles Leerhsen's ghostwritten hagiography *Trump: Surviving at the Top*, published in 1990, which features the future 45th American president juggling with an apple in front of a classic Magrittean blue-sky-with-white-clouds background. A cursory look in any bookshop at book covers featuring Magritte works demonstrates the diverse range of contexts and genres in which his works seem able to signify. While Magritte, like many Surrealist artists, is often used to illustrate science-fiction works (such as the 1965 novel *Fifth Planet* by Fred and Geoffrey Hoyle, an astrophysicist and his son, which features Magritte's *The Flavour of Tears* of 1948; the 2004 short story collection *Innocents Aboard* by Gene Wolfe, with the cover illustration of Magritte's *The Castle of the Pyrénées* of 1949; and an American paperback edition of H. G. Wells's *The Invisible Man*, which features Magritte's iconic bowler-hatted man), his adaptability extends to many other genres. The bowler-hatted man is also found on Lynda Resnick's *Rubies in the Orchard: The POM Queen's Secrets to Marketing Just About Anything* (2010). John Berger's *Ways of Seeing* uses for its cover *The Key of Dreams* (1930); Christopher Norris's *The Deconstructive Turn: Essays in the Rhetoric of Philosophy* features *Evening Falls* (1964); while the first edition of Brigid Brophy's 1969 experimental airport waiting-lounge novel *In Transit* features on its cover *The Black Flag* (1936–7), with its mysterious flying craft.

The wide generic significance of Magritte's art (from business advice books to art, philosophy, comedy and politics, and in spheres more conventionally seen as exclusive of each other, like high and popular art and culture) makes him unique among modern painters and problematizes from the outset his relationships with the various traditions that comprise Surrealism. His transcultural and crossmedial versatility was as useful in the high-modernist interwar European contexts of 1927, when Magritte began painting the pictures that would establish his iconic status, as it is in the radically different global orders of 2019. The continuing relevance of Magritte's works in public and popular fields is furthermore accompanied by (and reinforced in) their consistently strong exhibition profile: major retrospectives in recent years include MoMA's 'Magritte: The Mystery of the Ordinary, 1926–1938' (2013–14) and the Centre Pompidou's 'René Magritte, la trahison des images' (2016–17). 'Magritte' clearly remains a commodity with significant contemporary currency. He is a powerfully marketable product: a concept packaged within a lexicon of recognizable images with multiple potential applications, and a body of work open to continual display and curatorial renegotiation, made accessible and coherent for popular and critical consumption. The rough edges that don't quite fit the marketing concept (but which insist in the form of narratives and works that deviate, slightly disturbingly, from the critically established 'real' or 'familiar' Magritte) are often smoothed out in exhibitions, their differences assimilated, enforcing a particular set of narratives to account for and explain him and his work.

Yet this appearance of a 'consistent' Magrittean oeuvre masks the key way in which it effectively operates – the quality that enables his work to signify in such a variety of contexts. We might argue, first, that the popular and critical success of Magritte's oeuvre lies precisely in its inconsistency, the differences within its repetitiveness. Such inconsistency is evident in his varied, canonically problematic periods of productivity – such as his Cubist, sunlit or Vache periods – which remain marginal to the critically established and publicly celebrated central body of work, as well as in his use of media other than the familiar paintings – illustrations, objects, photography and even film (the latter work receiving, as yet, little critical attention). Similarly, Magritte's theoretical writings, many of them only recently translated into English, move well beyond philosophical explorations of representation and reality, originality and repetition, to include elements of Heideggerian thought, explorations of existentialism and communism, discussions of psychoanalysis (or rather arguments against it) and other intellectual preoccupations usually regarded by critics as diversions from the concerns of the 'real' Magritte. Second, we might note that Magritte's art is curiously resistant to metaphysical theorization. His works consistently refuse to be explained through the notion of some kind of transcendental condition outside reality – whether that transcendental is conceived as residing in the unconscious of the artist or the viewer, or as a divinely ordered space outside that of the real world. Indeed, many of his works actively construct reality itself as a kind of illusion beyond which there seems to be nothing, and insist that the elements and objects that make up reality – roses, trombones, apples, furniture, shaving equipment – signify not the presence of some order of experience beyond their materiality, but merely themselves, in all their materiality. Indeed, Magritte suggests that even the words we use to describe and define things and experiences are slippery, forms of deception that assume their own material qualities, sometimes negating themselves in the process: *une pipe* becoming *unpipe* as *un président* may become *unpresident*.

The version of 'Magritte' we are familiar with has, of course, been solidified by many biographical accounts. These include a number of publications by Magritte's friends and colleagues, including the first monograph on Magritte in 1943, written by Marcel Mariën under the guidance of Magritte; the writings of Magritte's close lifelong friends such as the poet Louis Scutenaire's

1947 monograph *René Magritte*; and the French art critic and former
Surrealist Patrick Waldberg's *René Magritte*, published in 1965 by
the Brussels-based Surrealist publication house of the Belgian poet,
collagist and editor André De Rache.

   While translations of these works are only gradually appearing,
biographies by leading art historians continue to familiarize
new anglophone audiences with Magritte and his works. These
include Suzi Gablik's *Magritte*, which was first published in 1970 in
Britain (1972 in America) and reissued in 1985; A. M. Hammacher's
Magritte, published in 1974 and frequently reprinted in subsequent
decades; and Harry Torczyner's *René Magritte: The True Art
of Painting* (1979), which draws on Torczyner's long-standing
friendship with the artist and is structured around thematically
ordered quotations. David Sylvester's 1992 monograph follows from
his curation of the Tate Gallery's 1969 Magritte retrospective, which
led the Menil Foundation in Houston to invite Sylvester and Sarah
Whitfield to produce in 1992–4 the five-volume Magritte *catalogue
raisonné* (with Whitfield and Michael Raeburn adding a sixth
volume of *Newly Discovered Works* in 2012).[3]

   Further important insights into Magritte's biography have been
offered by Michel Draguet's *Magritte* (2014) and collections of his
writings such as the *Écrits complets* (Complete Writings) – edited
by Magritte's friend the Belgian poet André Blavier and published
by Flammarion in 1979 – and the 2017 English translation of
Selected Writings, edited by Kathleen Rooney and Eric Plattner.
However, a number of aspects of his life remain (as George Melly
put it in a review of Sylvester's 1992 monograph) a 'mystery'.[4]
Accounts of Magritte's life are built upon a shifting ground of facts,
from the many vague or overlapping narratives established by
Magritte himself, to information gleaned from sources like Marcel
Mariën's 1983 autobiography, to documentary evidence, much of
it unverifiable or contested, of Belgian Surrealist activity. Each
source seems to open, rather than fill, gaps in knowledge. Magritte

and his friends consciously shaped, and sometimes fictionalized, his biographical legacy, moving between real and fake events and encounters and creating in the process an additional motivation for the fascination of subsequent generations with Magritte. These fictionalizations of his life not only shape his biography, they have become a fundamental part of it. Rather than hampering our understanding of Magritte, they have opened new ways of approaching his life and work, such as Vincent Zabus' *Magritte: This is Not a Biography* (2017), which offers fictional settings as entry points to Magritte's life and work, and my own *This is Magritte* (2016) in collaboration with the artist Iker Spozio, which maps some of the oscillations of Magritte's life between fact and fiction.

This book will add a new dimension to these already existing biographical approaches, offering a particular focus on events and experiences in Magritte's childhood and youth – all indicated by Magritte in his own writings and comments – in order to broaden the biographical and contextual frames in relation to which his art is conventionally considered. It will also introduce mass- and popular-cultural elements – key and influential aspects of Magritte's childhood experience – into the field of analysis. These elements centre on the significance of a key space, the place du Manège in Charleroi, Belgium, as a locus of popular entertainments in the influential arenas of the fairground, the circus, the cinema, the conjuring act and (linking these together) the carnivalesque. Each of these elements provides a context both distinct from and closely related to the others, in which different dimensions of the key themes of Magritte's art may be discerned, allowing us to see that art from new perspectives and to perceive in its forms and repetitions new kinds of significance.

Magritte's works are instantly recognizable because they operate with an idiosyncratic personal language of visual signs, the meanings of which are sufficiently superficially obscure to provoke a variety of critical interpretative responses and attempts to decode them.

If we situate the works in such deep historical contexts, these signs take on new resonances that enable us better to understand their biographical significance, and thus to read them in terms of their aesthetic importance within the frames that Magritte's art constructs. This book will explore the young artist's initial meeting with his future spouse and accomplice Georgette Berger in Charleroi in 1914 as a specific and crucially foundational moment in his youth. Until now, while both Magritte himself and his various scholars have mentioned this in the context of a budding affair, none have yet invested the encounter with further significance. But just like the revelation of a magic trick that is performed before our eyes, we must not merely see this moment but attend to it, in order to see its deeper, more extensive relevance – a relevance that will on one level allow us to flesh out some of the key moments in Magritte's little-known childhood and on another afford us significant new anchoring points for analysis of the iconographic sources and contexts of his later artistic production.

Magritte's Early Years

René-François-Ghislain Magritte was born on 21 November 1898 (a 'honeymoon baby', as his parents had married on 2 March of that year) in the town of Lessines, in the Walloon area of Belgium, roughly halfway between Charleroi and the North Sea. James Thrall Soby notes that the 'differences in cultural heritage between the Flemish and the Walloons are complicated . . . it is perhaps enough to note that René Magritte, born and raised in the Walloon country, was more susceptible to French influence than his Flemish colleagues.'[5] While the occupation of his mother Régine is noted on the marriage certificate as 'modiste' (a milliner), she was a housewife at the time of his birth (at 19 rue de la Station, Lessines). His father's occupation is recorded there and in subsequent

René on the lap of his mother, Régine Bertinchamps, 1899, photograph.

mentions as 'voyageur de commerce' (commercial traveller), but on Magritte's birth certificate Léopold is described as a 'marchand tailleur' (merchant tailor).[6] It is unclear whether these were two different jobs. A few years later he was working in the edible oil trade, as a representative for the margarine manufacturer Cocoline. Around 1915 he was representing the manufacturers of Maggi (which had produced its first stock cubes in 1908) and would establish his own stock cube factory in Brussels in 1917–18.[7] There may have been an earlier attempt to set up in business independently – an article in a local newspaper, *La Région de Charleroi*, from 27 October 1916 criticizes his product and insinuates fraud, stating: 'Leopold [*sic*] Magritte of Châtelet sold the "Vigor" broth contained in bottles with the label "Boiled guaranteed pure meat extract". However, analysis of this product has shown that it does not contain any part of meat extract.'[8] We might speculate on the influence of the father's questionable business enterprise on his son's future artistic analyses of the potential deceptions of words and images.

The Magritte family relocated frequently. In 1900 they moved to 185 chaussée de Fleurus in Gilly, where Magritte's brothers were born: Raymond in 1900 and Paul in 1902. While Raymond went on to become a successful businessman and maintained few ties to the family, Paul developed a close and lifelong relationship with his eldest brother. Nicknamed, as a young man, 'the Marquis' for his sartorial flair, Paul became a musician and collaborated on projects with René and his artist friends. He even joined Magritte in Paris from 1927 to 1930, and when they returned to Belgium the two brothers established, together with Georgette, the advertising firm Studio Dongo.

In 1904, when Magritte was five, the family moved to Châtelet and Magritte began attending the boys' middle school there in late 1905. In 1906 he is mentioned in the *Journal de Charleroi* for winning a prize in the yearly school competition,[9] and school records show that he was awarded a sixth prize in the fourth year for the following:

Prize for conduct and effort. Religious knowledge, average. French, honourable mention. Flemish, 5th prize. Arithmetic, 2nd prize. Natural sciences and hygiene, 2nd prize. History, 4th prize. Geography, 4th prize. Handwriting, 6th prize. Drawing, 3rd prize. Gymnastics, 6th prize. Music, 4th prize.[10]

In 1911 the Magrittes moved again, this time to a larger house built for them at 95 rue des Gravelles.

Following at least one earlier suicide attempt, Magritte's mother drowned herself in the river Sambre on 24 February 1912, less than a year after moving there. An announcement in the Charleroi newspaper *Le Rappel* on 25 February reads:

The disappearance is reported of Régine Bertinchamps, Mme Magritte, of 95 rue des Gravelles, Châtelet, who has not been seen since about 4.30 a.m. on Saturday. Age, 40; height, 1m 62; fairly stout build; black hair and eyebrows; clothes: red and white striped dressing-gown, white cotton nightdress with lace at the neck, black woollen stockings; gold wedding ring with the inscription 2-9-98 [a misprint of 2-3-98] inside. She was subject to depression and had indicated on several occasions her intention to put an end to her life.[11]

Her body was recovered on 12 March 1912. A newspaper report from the following day states:

It is a month ago that we reported the disappearance of Mrs Magritte, born Régine Bertinchamps, and certain circumstances had allowed the supposition that the unfortunate had put an end to her life. These presentiments

Paul, René and Raymond surround their father after the tragic death of their mother, 1912.

were well founded. In fact, yesterday morning, the body of the disappeared was retrieved from the water of the Sambre, behind the Agglomérés slag heap. The unfortunate's body was temporarily deposited in Mr Misonne's house until it was brought back to its home in rue des Gravelles.[12]

In November 1912, Magritte began his secondary education at the Athénée Royal Mixte in the nearby town of Charleroi. Not surprisingly given that year's traumatic events he performed badly, as noted in a letter of 1982 from his Préfet des Etudes to the Magritte *catalogues raisonnés*' editors David Sylvester and Sarah Whitfield: 'His first year there was up and down; the second verged on disaster, since his marks were less than 30 percent. Standing out among the ruins, however, a mark of 213 out of 250 for drawing. After that, we lost track of him.'[13] The young Magritte's more mischievous side is apparent in an article by A.-E. Degrange in *La Nouvelle Gazette de Bruxelles* from 9 January 1946, which records Magritte's pranks with his brother Paul: 'Young though he was, René Magritte practised Surrealism by hanging cats on the doorbells of respectable citizens. At the École Moyenne, he sought the bizarre through the macabre, and a work depicting a skull lit by a candle is cited as one of his first attempts.'[14] As Michel Draguet explains, the Magritte boys' escapades alienated them from their environment in Châtelet and had the unfortunate effect of generating a public perception that they were in some way responsible for the suicide of their mother.[15] It is clear from these descriptions that the Magritte children were, in rather unpleasant ways, something of a spectacle in the community. Perhaps as a consequence of such accusations, the family moved in March 1913 to 41 rue du Fort in the Walloon city in Charleroi.

The rue du Fort comprises traditional nineteenth-century, two- and three-storey red-brick houses, set directly on the pavement. The Athénée Royal Mixte was a twenty-minute walk from Magritte's house there, and to look after the children his father hired Jeanne Verdeyen, a governess who would later, in 1928, become his wife. The family's stay in Charleroi was relatively short – they returned to their Châtelet house in November 1914, and Magritte had by this time stopped attending school, following the German invasion, which began on 4 August. In November 1915 Magritte moved to Brussels, starting his life as a young bachelor and entering the Académie Royale des Beaux-Arts in October the following year. It is likely, given the proximity between Charleroi and Châtelet, that Magritte often visited Charleroi, both before and after actually residing there. The brevity of the family's Charleroi stay is also reflected in biographies which focus on the significant moment shortly preceding the move, of Magritte's mother's drowning in the river Sambre. This event (much to Magritte's chagrin, as he had little faith in psychoanalysis) is repeatedly used to contextualize his art in psychoanalytic terms, a tendency evident in critics like Ellen Handler Spitz, who notes the influence on Magritte's work of 'horror over the circumstances of a violent death' and the resulting 'post-traumatic state of mind'.[16]

Actual details of Magritte's childhood and youth, particularly the Charleroi years, are only sketchily outlined in biographies, which often focus on the key moments Magritte and Georgette themselves later, and rather briefly, cite as meaningful. Perhaps the most detailed account of his childhood is related in Magritte's 'Autobiographical Sketch', a cursory outline of a few moments in his life, written in oddly shifting tenses, published in the catalogue that accompanied his 1954 exhibition at the Palais des Beaux-Arts:

René-Francois-Ghislain MAGRITTE was born on 21st November 1898 in Lessines, in the province of Hainaut. His father, Léopold Magritte, and his mother, Régine Bertinchamps, were then living in a house which no longer exists. From his cradle, René Magritte saw helmeted men carrying the remains of a balloon which had crashed onto the roof of his family home.

In 1910, in Châtelet, where his parents have settled, René Magritte, who is twelve, colours in pictures and takes painting lessons. A teacher from a school in Dampremy, near Charleroi, comes once a week to give lessons to the young ladies of Châtelet. René Magritte is the sole representative (with the teacher) of the male sex in the improvised class, consisting of two rooms on the first floor of a sweet shop.

At this time, René Magritte spends his holidays in Soignies, with his aunt Flora, his grandma, his godmother Maria, and his godfather Firmin. He frequents an old cemetery, where, for the first time, he meets an artist who is working on the pictorial aspects of the old tombs in the sun for a local landowner.

René Magritte is then a pupil at the Athénée in Charleroi, where he astonishes his French teacher with his somewhat strange compositions. In 1912, his mother Régine is tired of life. She throws herself into the Sambre. In 1913, the family,

consisting of the father, René and his brothers Raymond
and Paul, move to Charleroi. There, in a *carousel-salon*,
René Magritte meets Georgette Berger, his future wife.[17]

The meeting with Georgette while riding a carousel is the last
moment of the narrative which takes place in a discernible (and
also, conveniently, pre-war) childhood. The 'Autobiographical
Sketch' then skips over the First World War to Magritte's
infrequent attendance of the Académie Royale des Beaux-Arts in
Brussels, and his family's move to Brussels in 1918.

Georgette-Marie-Florence Berger was born on 22 February
1901, in Marcinelle (across the river Sambre from Charleroi), a
coal-mining town that in 1977 became part of the municipality of
Charleroi. Her parents, Lia Payot and Florent-Joseph Berger, owned
a butcher/charcuterie shop in their home town. She recalled her
first meeting with Magritte:

> In Charleroi, where I spent my childhood, the annual fair
> was in progress. In the square in the upper part of the town,
> there was a covered-in roundabout: 'Come for a ride', said
> a very young man. After that, René and I met almost daily
> on the way to our respective schools. The 1914 war began . . .
> René went off to Brussels and I lost touch with him.[18]

Biographies note that the fair took place (apparently in August)
at the place du Manège, a lively urban arena of socializing and
entertainment and the locus of many of the key moments and
passages of Magritte's youth.[19] One of the main public spaces
for amusements in Charleroi, the place du Manège was only five
minutes' walk from his home and is located just off the rue Neuve,
where the Cinéma Bleu stood – another key formative place in
Magritte's youth, as will be discussed below. Magritte would often
have frequented the place du Manège after school. Its centrality to his

daily life is clear from Georgette bumping into him there during the fair, and his school grades point to somebody who, we might surmise, was often out and about in Charleroi rather than staying in studying.

The early twentieth-century giddiness and excitement associated with activities in and around the place can be gleaned from an article printed in 1904 in the *Gazette de Charleroi*:

> Decidedly, the people who are still bored in Charleroi are terribly difficult or singularly grumpy! Festivals are organized everywhere, in all neighbourhoods! Here in its turn is the place du Manège! This neighbourhood has had an extraordinarily rapid development! The houses were raised from the ground as if by enchantment, particularly in the boulevard Jacques Bertrand, and near the permanent Circus, around which many cafés and even private houses have emerged. Thanks to the regular evenings of the Circus, and to the Easter and August fairs, this district presents almost continually a great animation. The inhabitants want this to be redoubled, thanks to new festivals.[20]

The daily hustle and bustle of the place du Manège was enhanced further by the regular and long fairs held there. The Easter fairs were, according to Philippe Dimbourg, fifteen days long, while the August fair lasted the whole month.[21] Central to the place du Manège at the time was a *Sporting-Palace*, a large sports complex where for a general entry price of 50 cents visitors could use its popular roller-skating facilities – as the *Gazette de Charleroi* notes, 'the largest skating rink in Hainaut' – accompanied sometimes by 'Professor Nestor's presentation of his "éléphant patineur"' (Skating Elephant).[22]

Fairgrounds played important social, cultural and economic roles in late nineteenth- and early twentieth-century Belgium, which at the time was one of the wealthiest countries on the continent and had colonial interests in the Congo and (from 1916) Ruanda-Urundi (later Rwanda). Its densely populated industrial areas centred around the cities of Liège, Mons, Charleroi, Ghent, Antwerp and Brussels with, as Guido Convents notes, over 'seven million Belgians living on 30,000 square kilometers'.[23] A wealthy middle class (including the parents of both Magritte and Georgette) and a prosperous working class quickly established themselves in these urban areas, with a fast-growing number of small shop owners, publicans and brewers: 'successful popular feasts were appreciated and even explicitly asked for by the local middle class and industrialists.'[24] This rapidly developing bourgeois society attracted people to the towns, increasing business, and the tax received from travelling exhibits became an increasingly important revenue for local authorities.[25]

While in biographies of Magritte the detail of this last childhood moment grounds a straightforward but lifelong love and marriage (despite it being tempestuous at times and undermined by affairs on both sides), it elicits little further scholarly attention. Indeed, as noted above, it is the drowning of Magritte's mother that scholarship regards as the most significant influence on his later artistic production. But what if we look awry at this all-too-brief sketch of a childhood, and reposition this last moment of the fairground encounter – in 1913, riding a carousel on the cusp of both grand historical changes and its author's (and his partners) adolescence and adulthood – as central to an understanding of Magritte's work? We are presented with a brief moment whose poetic imagery emerges from the (characteristically modern) fleetingness of pleasure associated with the circular, giddy, elevating motion of carousels and the migrant transitoriness of the fairs of which they were a part; and we might trace the persistence of memories of this moment in the lives of René and Georgette, whose lifelong partnership (with all its ups and downs) was seemingly sealed at that moment. Moreover, this giddiness contradicts the more conventional grey and drab environment into which biographers like David Sylvester often place the artist. As he writes:

> Magritte was born and grew up in Hainaut, the province of Belgium known as the Black Country, something of an inferno then (a limbo now), a grey country, drab land under leaden sky, dark slopes of slag heaps here and there. Often the mystery in Magritte's paintings, a mystery found in the banal, not the beyond, is a celebration of Hainaut's greyness.[26]

But what if Magritte's childhood in the 'Black Country' was less drab than Sylvester implies and was, instead, shot through with colourful, celebratory and even carnivalesque spaces and experiences that were just as influential on his artistic work and development? What if we follow the trail of the travelling circuses, carnivals and magic shows that regularly bustled in the place du Manège – lifting the bourgeois man's bowler hat which so defined Magritte's self-representation and images, to reveal the trickster and magician underneath – and trace a biography that is not linear but circular, like a carousel ride, consisting of moments of return and turning back? Looking around the spatial, historical and cultural fringes of this shared life, this foundational and transitory moment provides a still point from which to flesh out the all-too-patchy biographical details of Magritte's childhood, and thence to construct an alternative narrative of his work, complementing rather than contradicting previous ones. The significance of the various places and spaces of such amusement in Magritte's childhood may offer further textures to his biography, while also enhancing critical understanding of his works, offering layers of a deep context, so to speak, to be found in the popular and folk-cultural environs of his early life.

We need then to turn – and repeatedly return, carousel-like – to a key biographical moment, to the meeting of two young people, a fourteen-year-old boy, who moved to Charleroi in March 1913, and a twelve-year-old girl. This meeting foretold multiple encounters, enabling us retrospectively to shift our perspective on Magritte's art. Magritte once noted that reality was 'absurd' and 'incoherent', and that coherence is imposed upon it by bourgeois ideology;[27] trying to present a biographically linear narrative would, in a similar way, be attempting the impossible. Memories and narratives are fragmented, repetitive, circular rather than linear. Faded by the effects of time, lost evidence and the subjectivity of perceptions, they may offer structure to a story but not necessarily insights into what that story has produced. In turn, exploring a biographical moment – a specific space, seemingly insignificant in the Magritte narrative beyond its romantic connotations – may allow us to excavate depths in this life, as well as new layers in his artistic production.

1
Independent Beginnings:
Shaping Belgian Surrealism

As noted earlier, Magritte stopped attending school after Germany invaded Belgium on 4 August 1914, and the family returned to their Châtelet house in November. A year later, Magritte moved alone to a boarding house in Brussels. Very little is known about what he did there – he is recorded as being a 'dessinateur' (draughtsman) in the Brussels population register – but (as we will see later) cinema visits may well have been one of his main activities, significantly shaping his subsequent artistic work. Magritte himself provided little information about this period. In an interview with Michel Georis in 1962, he briefly looks back on this time in Brussels: 'During the 1914–18 War, I enrolled at the Academy in Brussels. I stayed there two years. I lived alone at the time in a very free and easy boarding-house and seldom attended classes.'[1] Records show that he actually enrolled in the Académie Royale des Beaux-Arts in 1916. He rarely frequented the academy, not least as it was regularly closed during the war for many reasons, including a lack of coal for heating. While it was difficult to acquire books from the depleted wartime library, students could buy postcard reproductions of photographs and artworks from the Co-opérative Artistique, which also provided prospectuses for unaffordable art books. It is perhaps worth considering this early exposure to art through reproductions in the wider context of Magritte's later concerns with originality and reproduction, ranging from his later copying of his own works and pictures printed in encyclopaedias such as *Larousse*, to the explorations of relations between reality and copy, model and reproduction within the works themselves.

After a short period in the boarding house Magritte once again took up residence with his father and his two brothers, who had moved to Brussels in 1916 or 1917. A description by Charles Alexandre (1896–1990), a close friend and fellow student at the time, reveals much about the Magritte family dynamics:

> The whole family was at table and Magritte introduced me [to]: 'Popaul, my brother, who's an imbecile, because he doesn't give a damn for anyone, Raymond even more so; that's my dad, that's dad's mistress', he said, pointing to the housekeeper (I've no idea if it was true), 'and that's his bastard son.' And then his father leapt up in a rage and shouted at him: 'Imbecile, lout . . . insulting your family like that'.[2]

The family eventually moved into a large town house in Schaerbeek, on the outskirts of Brussels, with his father earning a decent income producing stock cubes on the premises, keeping the family fairly comfortable during the war period. Alexandre notes that

> The house had three floors. Not all the rooms were inhabited. On the top floor there were two or three rooms in which there were easels and little else. And Magritte had this top floor more or less all to himself. In the corner of one room there was a pile of old clothes, and when he was tired he would go and lie down on it. I never saw a bed of his; I don't know where he slept. He must have had a bedroom somewhere, I suppose, but I never saw it. We used to go straight up to the studio and then we would sit and smoke the poisonous wartime tobacco and talk about poetry and philosophy.[3]

Between 1919 and 1925 Magritte established what would become long-term relations with key figures and lifelong thematic and philosophical interests and positions significant for his artistic development. By 1919 he was sharing a studio with Pierre-Louis Flouquet (1900–1967) and had become friends with the Bourgeois brothers, Victor (1897–1962) and Pierre (1898–1976). Flouquet was a painter and Victor a budding architect, while Pierre was a poet and writer. All three would, together with Magritte, be at the heart of avant-garde artistic life in Brussels in the coming decade. Magritte was exposed around 1919 to his first truly modern art movement, Futurism, through reproduction in an exhibition catalogue probably given to him by Pierre Bourgeois. Several disparate encounters and events that year eventually led to the establishment of the Brussels Surrealist group, the first group manifestation of Surrealism in Belgium. The Bourgeois brothers included Magritte on the editorial board for their review of modern art and architecture, *Au volant*, the first issue appearing in January 1919. In December of that year Victor opened the Centre d'Art in Brussels with Aimé Declercq, including poster designs by Magritte in its opening exhibition.

Another artistic movement that proved formative for Magritte was Dada, and his first contact with this work was in part down to the efforts of the Belgian Dadaist Clément Pansaers (1885–1922) to establish links with French Dadaists. Pansaers was originally the editor of the periodical *Résurrection* and established contact in early 1919 with the founding Dadaist Tristan Tzara (1896–1963), a Romanian-born artist then living in Paris who, in his *Bulletin Dada* (number 6, 1919), dubbed Pansaers the 'Dada President' in Belgium. Pansaers also corresponded with the French artist Francis Picabia (1879–1953), collaborating with him on *Littérature*, a journal published initially from 1919 to 1921 by the French writers Philippe Soupault (1897–1990), Louis Aragon (1897–1982) and the future Surrealist leader André Breton (1896–1966). *Littérature* can

René and Georgette Magritte, Pierre and Henri Flouquet and an unknown friend, 1920, photograph.

be regarded as the starting point of Surrealism per se. Around the same time, Edouard Léon Théodore Mesens (1903–1971), the sixteen-year-old son of a pharmaceuticals wholesaler, was also in contact with Tzara in Paris.

Mesens, a major figure in Belgium's literary avant-garde, had received a good musical education and between the ages of 14 and 21 set to music numerous texts and poems by writers such as François Coppée, Guillaume Apollinaire and Rabindranath Tagore. He recalled meeting Magritte and Pierre Flouquet in 1920 in 'an establishment pompously styled "Centre d'Art"'.[4] Magritte's contributions to the centre's opening exhibition showed a variety of influences from the then-fashionable Cubist and Futurist styles, alongside traces of German and Flemish Expressionism. In an unpublished manuscript Mesens comments on Magritte's appearance at the time:

> He seemed to us extremely elegant. He had suits made to measure which were so nipped-in at the waist that they gave him the look of a pregnant girl. Every Sunday his father crimped his hair with curling-tongs. He also at that time wore button boots with pearl-grey cloth uppers and crowned this whole get-up with an enormous wide-brimmed Borsalino: a first-communion cake under a cheese-dome![5]

Mesens, who had moved to Paris in 1921, was instrumental in acquainting Magritte and other figures in the Belgian avant-garde with those artists and writers in France who were at that time developing what would become Surrealism, including Tzara, Soupault, the Dadaist writer and artist Georges Ribemont-Dessaignes (1884–1974), Picabia, Marcel Duchamp (1887–1968) and the composer Erik Satie (1866–1925). Mesens also visited the first exhibition of the Paris-based American photographer Man Ray (1890–1976), soon to become another key Surrealist associate.

Through Mesens's Parisian contacts Magritte now had direct access to information about the Paris art world, and Mesens would often send Magritte journals, exhibition catalogues and other items, keeping his friend up to date about new developments in the Parisian avant-garde.

Mesens's discovery of the Dadaists and modern music, particularly the work of Erik Satie, was in turn influential on Magritte. Dadaism and modern music were closely related – Satie introduced Mesens to Dada and initiated his and Magritte's contributions to the final issue of Picabia's journal *391*, for which Mesens became the 'agent in Brussels'.[6] Mesens recalled returning to Brussels to be 'reviled by his friends, with the exception of Magritte, for having hobnobbed with Dadaists'.[7] He met Satie in 1921 when the latter came to Brussels for the first performance of *Socrate*, his 1919 work for voice and piano, and Satie looked after Mesens when he paid his first visit to Paris. While many of his Parisian friends already regarded Dada as a thing of the past (modernist fashions being highly mutable), the continuing significance of the movement in Belgium after 1921 can be clearly seen in the first journals established by Magritte and Mesens, namely *Oesophage* (which published a single issue in 1925) and *Marie* (which ran for three issues in 1926). Both are heavily imbued with the Dada spirit. Mesens and Magritte became representatives of Dada in Belgium, but they were only in touch with one Belgian Dadaist: the painter Paul Joostens (1889–1960).

As mentioned, the first avant-garde influence on Magritte was Italian Futurism, the art of modern dynamism and speed championed from around 1909 by Filippo Tommaso Marinetti (1876–1944). Magritte's early paintings, none of which have survived, seem to have imitated Futurist style. He states in a letter of 23 February 1967 to Phil Mertens: 'It was a pure pleasure to paint in that style and I didn't keep anything; nothing remains of my futurist exercises.'[8] Soon after their initial enthusiasm, however,

Magritte and Mesens distanced themselves from the Futurists, not only for aesthetic reasons but because of the movement's close association with the rise of Italian fascism. Mesens commented on their relation to Futurism:

> It was not long before we were shocked by their acceptance of 'modern life' in all its brutality. What seemed to us totally incompatible with our humanitarian sympathies at the time was the conquering, imperialistic spirit of the Futurists, the very spirit which was a harbinger of Italian Fascism.[9]

Another key moment for Magritte, once more in connection to Mesens, was his first encounter with the art of Giorgio de Chirico (1888–1978). Again, conflicting narratives exist around this moment. In one version it coincides with Magritte meeting the Brussels writer Marcel Lecomte (1900–1966), who remained close to Magritte throughout his life – Lecomte's publications, such as his volume of prose poems *Applications* (1925), often included Magritte's illustrations. Magritte tells us in his 1954 'Autobiographical Sketch':

> In 1922, René Magritte became acquainted with Marcel Lecomte. The painter's experiments were beginning to achieve some results. Lecomte showed Magritte a photograph of a picture by Chirico, *The Love Song* (1914), and the painter could not hold back his tears.[10]

However, Mesens tells a different story with different dates. He notes a meeting with Magritte in autumn 1924 when the pair discussed a possible collaboration on the Dada journal *391* and their post-Dada publication *Oesophage*:

> Very shortly afterwards, a reproduction of [De Chirico's]
> 'The Love Song' happened to fall into our hands. We were
> bewitched. A few days later, Magritte discovered in a second-
> hand bookshop a *Valori Plastici* booklet devoted to the same
> painter. We were overcome by an unparalleled emotion.[11]

Mesens's dating seems to better explain the evident change in
Magritte's style in 1925, but the two men closely collaborated with
Lecomte, who may well have introduced them both to De Chirico's
work. According to Sylvester and Whitfield, Mesens's papers give
'the location as the Paris review *Les Feuilles libres*. Now, this review
contained a single monochrome reproduction of ["The love song"]
in its issue for May–June 1923.'[12] In May 1924 André de Ridder
(1888–1961) and Paul-Gustave Van Hecke (1887–1967) published an
article on De Chirico by René Crevel in their art periodical *Sélection*.
The six reproductions of De Chirico's works illustrating the article
included *The Love Song*. Mesens was listed as a member of the
editorial board of *Sélection*, which suggests that Magritte and his
friends probably knew of De Chirico months before the article was
published and may even have helped commission it.[13] It is clear that
sometime around the second half of 1923 Magritte encountered a
reproduction of De Chirico's *The Love Song* and that through this
encounter the artistic potential of painting stagings and screens
became clear to him. From then on, he always emphasized the
importance of De Chirico's art in his development as a painter.

The career trajectories of Mesens and Magritte continued to
be closely interdependent, albeit not without mutual qualms.
Mesens created opportunities for Magritte's work to be seen, while
Magritte's work largely facilitated Mesens's successes as an art
dealer and gallerist. In 1927 Mesens directed the Galerie L'Époque
(owned by Paul-Gustave Van Hecke) in Brussels, in which Magritte
exhibited; he was also editor of the 1929 special issue *Variétés*,
one of the most significant collaborations between the Belgian

and French Surrealists, and, in 1929, the review *Violette Nozières*. He became Magritte's art dealer in 1931 and was instrumental in introducing him to British audiences. However, in 1924 Magritte made the acquaintance of the poet, critic and art dealer Camille-Constant-Ghislain Goemans (1900–1960) and Paul Nougé (1895–1967), a biochemist working in a clinical biology laboratory in Brussels. The same year Magritte, Mesens, Goemans and Lecomte together published a Dada-inspired pamphlet that contained the announcement of a forthcoming review to be called *Période*. At this time, as Mesens commented, 'something rather obscure happened: the group split in two' – a split most apparent in the ensuing duel between two factions of the avant-garde, fought out through competing journal publications.[14] While Magritte and Mesens published the Dada-oriented *Oesophage* in March 1925, followed by *Marie*, Goemans, Lecomte and Nougé published *Correspondance*, distancing themselves from Dada and moving towards Surrealism.

Oesophage and *Correspondance* divided the avant-garde community in Brussels in ways reminiscent of the earlier split between the Dadaists and the Surrealists in Paris. The only issue of *Oesophage*, heavily influenced by Picabia (who at the time, together with Tzara, was most fervently hostile to Surrealism) survived for only a single issue. Its avowedly Dadaist spirit was seen as regressive by those more interested in the fresh potential of Surrealism as promoted by *Correspondance*. Nevertheless, the extent to which both journals were anchored in Dadaism is clear from the list of contributors and the character of the contributions. *Oesophage*, with a layout reminiscent of Dada reviews such as *Dada* or *Merz*, opened with 'Les 5 Commandements', which finishes with the Dadaist call: '"Hop-là, Hop-là" t'elle est notre devise' ('Hop-là, Hop-là', this is our slogan). The issue included poems by the German artist Hans Arp (1886–1966) and by Tzara, and illustrations of artworks by Paul Joostens and the Germans Max Ernst (1891–1976) and Kurt Schwitters (1887–1948). It also featured

Picabia's *superréaliste* drawing *Hyperpoetry: Rimbaud Thermometer* (1924), which was framed by Tzara's comment: 'La merdre, c'est du réalisme; le surréalisme, c'est l'odeur de la merdre' (Realism is shit; Surrealism is the stink of shit). At the same time, *Oesophage* also voiced reservations about Dadaism: 'Nous protesterons énergiquement contre toutes les décadences: l'érudition, la Chartreuse de Parma, le dadaïsme et ses succédanés' (We will protest energetically against all decadence: erudition, [Stendhal's novel] the Charterhouse of Parma, Dadaism and its successors).

The first issue of *Correspondance* was published on 22 November 1924. The three avant-garde poets publishing the journal, Nougé, Goemans and Lecomte, began meeting regularly to discuss new books by French writers including Breton, Jean Paulhan (1884–1968), Marcel Proust (1871–1922), Paul Éluard (1895–1952) and Paul Valéry (1871–1945). The essays published in *Correspondance* emerged out of these discussions, and the publication was regarded by Paul Nougé as a 'reply to an investigation on modernism'.[15] *Correspondance* pursued a new, clearly Surrealist-influenced direction, its initial appearance coinciding historically with the official birth of Surrealism in 1924, the publication of André Breton's first *Manifesto of Surrealism*, and with the establishment of the Bureau de Recherches Surréalistes in Paris, which had opened on 15 October 1924.[16] The rivalry between *Oesophage* and *Correspondance* concluded with the formation of a Brussels-based Belgian Surrealist group including at its core Magritte, Mesens, Nougé, Goemans and the composer and conductor André Souris (1899–1970). The entente was solidified by their co-publishing three collectively signed texts in October and November 1926, and their collaboration on the final issue of *Marie* – titled *Adieu à Marie* – edited by Nougé and published in February or March 1927.

Another key member of this new group was Louis Scutenaire (1905–1987). He was born in a small village near Lessines called Ollignies, and moved with his family to Brussels in 1924. Scutenaire

studied law at the Université Libre and was called to the bar
in 1930, the year he married Irène Hamoir (1906–1994), a writer
employed as a journalist at the International Court of Justice in
The Hague. Working as a criminal lawyer from 1931 to 1944,
Scutenaire applied successfully in 1941 to enter the civil service
as a *conseiller* (advisor) in the Ministry of the Interior. He began
publishing his poetry and writings from 1927 onwards, at first
as Jean-Victor Scutenaire, then as Jean Scutenaire, and after
the Second World War as Louis Scutenaire. Magritte's lifelong
friendship with Scutenaire began in June 1927, following the
latter's initial contact with Nougé and Goemans. Scutenaire was
introduced to the rest of the group, including Mesens and Lecomte,
whom he met in one of their usual haunts, the Café Cirio at 18 rue
de la Bourse, near the stock exchange.

Shaping Belgian Surrealism

These friendships and collaborations forged a host of philosophical
and artistic positions that, while increasingly situated in relation
to French Surrealism, fundamentally differed from it – not least in
terms of the possibilities of aesthetic creativity. Together with his
Belgian friends, including the poet Nougé, Magritte developed a set
of ideas and practices about aesthetic productivity that effectively
rejected Breton's Surrealist focus on automatism, the dream and
the unconscious (and the resulting denigration of the importance
of conscious agency in relation to artistic productivity). Instead,
Magritte concentrated on producing clearly contra-automatist
images that foregrounded their constructedness and artifice.
Assuming this intellectual position was effectively a criticism,
and sometimes even a mockery, of Breton's belief (influenced by
his reading of Freud) in the centrality of unconscious motivations
to artistic production – the argument that writing and art could

directly tap into unconscious content and transmit it in some unmediated way.

The intellectual differences between Breton and the Belgian Surrealists (and specifically Magritte and Nougé) can be seen in the latter's adaptation of ideas developed by the French poet and philosopher Paul Valéry. One of Breton's key contributions to the theory of Surrealism was his notion of automatic writing, which Roger Rothman describes as a 'poetry of immediacy', conceived and intended as an unmediated language of spontaneity.[17] As Breton writes in the first *Manifesto of Surrealism* in 1924: 'the first sentence will come spontaneously, so compelling is the truth that with every passing second there is a sentence unknown to our consciousness which is only crying out to be heard.'[18] This emphasis on poetic spontaneity, which elevates the unconscious to the position of prime creator, stands in stark contrast to Valéry's conception of poetry as what Rothman calls a 'hyperrationalized craft' – a conception upon which Nougé and, following him, Magritte, extensively drew. Valéry was interested in what Rothman calls the 'notion of artifice', that is, 'the inherently deceptive nature of linguistic communication and, with it, an uncompromising assault on the notion of literary sincerity'.[19] For Valéry, writes Rothman,

> nothing guaranteed the authenticity of a poem – not trance states, not inspiration, not the will to the naïve [which Breton identified, for example, in the art of children]. Insofar as one operates within the realm of language, one engages in a practice that is fundamentally at odds with the structure of thought . . . there is simply no way to bridge the gap between the conventions of language and the operations of thought.[20]

In short, there is no direct connection between reality (or the unconscious, which Breton conceived as an enhanced form of 'reality') and the languages (verbal or pictorial) available to the artist. Valéry therefore insisted on adherence to classical conventions of rhetoric and its force, its ability to influence the reader. The application of classicism involved a 'certain recognition of the conventionality of the language it employs' in order not to describe the world but to cause an effect in the reader/viewer.[21] Most pointedly, Valéry argued that a Romantic who truly understood how art worked would be in danger of becoming a classic – thus inverting the ideological opposition that organized much nineteenth-century French (and, indeed, European) thought about distinct kinds of artist.

Paul Nougé deliberately aligned himself with, and built upon, Valéry's position, asserting that the poet is locked into language and its rules – any critique of or influence on reality cannot be achieved through some sort of direct access to that reality but needs to emerge instead from the self-reflective manipulation of the rules and conventions of the medium, whether linguistic or pictorial. As Valéry notes: 'A work of art is always a *fake* (which is to say *a fabrication in which one cannot connect an author* as the only actor in the process). It is the product of a diverse collaboration.'[22] The fakeness of a poem is its honesty, while sincerity claimed by processes such as the automatic ones is the greatest lie. The underlying relevance of these ideas to an understanding of Magritte's art will be developed in the discussions below.

Amid these debates, Belgian Surrealists were engaged in two processes: defining their own intellectual convictions and concerns; and differentiating themselves from arguments developed, and positions occupied, by Breton and his group in Paris. Magritte mapped out key elements of this Belgian Surrealist intellectual position in his theoretical writing 'Les Mots et les images' (Words and Images, 1929), which was published together with Breton's *Second Manifesto of Surrealism* in the twelfth and final issue of the French *La Révolution surréaliste* (15 December 1929). 'Les Mots et les images' can be read as a counter-manifesto to Breton's *Second*

Manifesto. The latter was itself, in part, an attempt to respond to
Nougé's reservations about Bretonian Surrealism as it had been
defined in the first *Manifesto*, and to reassert the importance of
Freudian thought and the unconscious. Despite expressing concern
regarding automatism and the interpretation of dreams, Breton
maintains in the *Second Manifesto* that 'surrealism believes Freudian
criticism to be the first and only one with a really solid basis.'[23] In
contrast, Magritte's 'Les Mots et les images' eschews any mention of
automatism and presents instead eighteen axioms on signification
– the relations between words and images and the things they
represent – in an 'attempt to systematize a practice and in so doing
define a position'.[24] Magritte's axioms on representation seem
to stand as a counter-argument to Breton's faith in the ability of
psychoanalysis to penetrate the unconscious and accurately record
its workings in automatist artworks. He insists that 'everything tends
to suggest that there is little connection between an object and what
represents it.'[25] This is clearly the position of the Belgian Surrealists
who, in the words of Magritte's mentee and fellow artist Marcel
Mariën (1920–1993), accused Breton of 'confound[ing] with diligence
thoughts with language'.[26] Following Valéry's arguments on poetic
artifice, the Belgians argued contra Breton, that the unconscious is
unavoidably mediated by and has to pass through language, and that
consequently whatever the unconscious presents is subject (in its
necessary encoding in words) to linguistic uncertainty, slippage and
ambiguity, offering no grounding in truth or certainty.

'Les Mots et les images' and Magritte's famous 1929 painting
of a pipe in *The Treachery of Images* both elaborate, in closely
connected ways, on the important implications of the difference
between signifier and signified, exploring the relationship
between a representation and its visual and verbal construction
and challenging Breton's focus on a representation being a
(direct) expression of the unconscious. This refusal of Bretonian
Surrealism's emphasis on the unconscious and the dreamlike

is recalled in André Souris' assertion (in 1968) that the Belgian Surrealist group's aim was not to 'go into the fantastic, the dream, or the unconscious, but to try to give new and poetic effects to ready-made objects, objects that exist'. Souris continued (in one of many critical attempts to impose definitions on Magritte): 'I think that is how you can define Magritte's painting.'[27]

Souris' point emphasizes that the fundamental and distinct intellectual differences between Breton's French Surrealist colleagues and the Belgians did not shift over the years. While significant collaborations between the two groupings were sometimes achieved, particularly in relation to various attempts over the years to establish an international Surrealism, they also repeatedly broke down, due fundamentally to clashes over these original and apparently irreconcilable intellectual differences over the workings of language. These tensions are clear from the 1934 collaboration (after Éluard negotiated a re-establishment of contact between Breton and Magritte) on the 'first international surrealist exhibition ever (camouflaged, under the auspices of the magazine *Minotaure*, as an "Exposition Minotaure")'.[28] Breton's lecture 'Qu'est-ce que le surréalisme?' (What is Surrealism?) was delivered in Brussels on 1 June 1934, on the occasion of this exhibition. It opened as follows:

The activity of our surrealist comrades in Belgium is closely allied with our own activity, and I am happy to be in their company this evening. Magritte, Mesens, Nougé, Scutenaire and Souris are among those whose revolutionary will – outside of all consideration of their agreement or disagreement with us on particular points – has been for us in Paris a constant reason for thinking that the surrealist project, beyond the limitations of space and time, can contribute to the efficacious reunification of all those *who do not despair of the transformation of the world and who wish this transformation to be as radical as possible.*[29]

This address altered the real relations to such an extent that André Souris felt he had been effectively conscripted to Breton's desired international Surrealism.[30]

Similar conflicts emerged later, with Breton's regrouping of international Surrealism after the war with the exhibition 'Le Surréalisme en 1947' (which was actually preceded by a show in Brussels, organized by Magritte, that ran from 15 December 1945 to 15 January 1946). In his catalogue essay 'Devant le rideau' (Before the Curtain), Breton objected to Magritte's concept of 'le surréalisme en plein soleil [Surrealism in broad daylight]' (and, to the ideas of the Belgian Surrealists in general) in near-derogatory terms: 'it is difficult not to see their behaviour as equivalent to that of a (backward) child who, to make sure that he has a pleasant day, conceives the bright idea of fixing the needle of the barometer at "set fair."'[31] Sylvester comments that Magritte perceived this attack as 'an excommunication'.[32] In response to it, Nougé wrote about Breton's show in 'Les Points sur les signes' (Points on signs) – his preface to the catalogue of Magritte's 1948 Brussels exhibition – in terms that relegate Bretonian Surrealism to the category of a mystical delusion:

> And they pretend to recognize the theoretical expression of a purely experimental thought in pretentious and incoherent ravings in which sordid superstitions and milky mysticisms are tangled together. Appearing here are tarots, horoscopes, premonitions, hysteria, objective chance, black masses, kabbalah, voodoo rites, ossified folklore, ceremonial magic. There is no longer any question of citing André Breton, who deserves to be outcast.[33]

Musical Differences

If the rejection and indeed debunking of the authority of automatism, the unconscious and dream imagery over French Surrealist practice was one key aspect of the difference between French and Belgian groups, the importance of music was another. The insistent presence of musical instruments, notation and performers in Magritte's works testifies to a significant difference between his art and thought (and that of his Belgian Surrealist friends) and the conceptions of Surrealism held by Breton and those around him in Paris. Indeed, Breton was notoriously disinterested in music, stating in his 1928 essay 'Surrealism and Painting':

> Auditive images, in fact, are inferior to visual images not only in clarity but also in strictness and, with all due respect to a few megalomaniacs, they are not destined to strengthen the idea of human greatness. So may night continue to descend upon the orchestra, and may I . . . be left with open eyes, or with closed eyes in broad daylight, to my silent contemplation.[34]

Magritte and the Brussels Surrealists were, on the other hand, steeped in music, as is clear from the early Brussels Surrealist publications. In 1926 alone two issues of *Correspondance* were entitled 'Musique', and included, together with works by Goemans and Marcel Lecomte, contributions from the musicologist Paul Hooreman (1903–1977) and the composer and conductor André Souris. In the same year, departing from their earlier attachment to Dada in order to move towards Surrealism, Mesens and Magritte published (as noted earlier) the final issue of the journal *Marie*. *Adieu à Marie* demonstrated that a strong and talented Belgian Surrealist group existed, producing work in a variety of media including poetry, painting, photography and music. The issue included an essay on music by Souris, which, Sylvester argues, was 'highly significant as an indicator of that group's contempt for one of the prejudices of the French Surrealist group – the sanctions imposed within it upon musical activity'.[35] Sylvester also points to a letter from Magritte to Harry Torczyner (1910–1998), written towards the end of his life, in which Magritte states that 'he had always been inhibited in his friendship with Breton by the difficulty he found in getting on with someone who didn't like music.'[36]

The significance of music for Magritte is further emphasized by several personal factors. His brother Paul was a professional musician and had been taught piano by Mesens, with whom he collaborated on musical pieces for which Magritte drew the coversheets. Magritte also loved the music of Satie and other composers (recalling the importance of Satie during Mesens's first visit to Paris). Magritte's collaborator and spouse, Georgette, compiled an alphabetical list of his favourite composers and works, which indicates an expansive but also specific taste ranging from Albéniz and Albinoni to Vivaldi and Wagner.[37]

The Belgian Surrealists also held concert events, including one in January 1929 at Charleroi's stock exchange that involved a collaboration between Nougé, Magritte and Souris. It included an exhibition of eighteen paintings by Magritte and the concert itself, directed by Souris, which included works by composers from the 1910s and '20s, among them Arnold Schoenberg, Igor Stravinsky, Arthur Honegger and Darius Milhaud. The music was preceded with a lecture by Nougé that explicitly emphasized music's integral role in the artistic work of the Belgian Surrealist group, again distinguishing the group clearly from their Paris counterparts.[38]

The repudiation of automatism and the emphasis on music are two key ways in which Belgian Surrealism distinguished itself from the French variety and sought to define its own intellectual and aesthetic territories. The debates around these distinct positions defined some of the key contexts that exerted influence on Magritte throughout his artistic career and that more widely influenced the development of a distinctive Belgian Surrealist tradition. This was a tradition to which Magritte's art made a huge and long-term contribution, though he would at the same time retain his own idiosyncratic style and repertoire of motifs. The diverse significance of this style and these motifs to contemporary publishing and marketing has already been noted, but their origins can also be traced in Magritte's own involvement from early in his career with commercial enterprises that afforded financial relief to the young, struggling artist in 1920s Brussels.

2

From Commerce to Art

Parallel to Magritte's artistic development, his career from the early 1920s also took a commercial trajectory, an area of productivity with which he had a love–hate relationship but which would nevertheless closely interlace with his artistic work throughout his life. His artworks incorporated commercial elements and vice versa, to such an extent that disentangling artistic and commercial objects becomes near impossible.

Magritte started a full-time job as a designer at the wallpaper manufacturer Peters-Lacroix in Brussels in November 1921, on the strength of his training at the academy and his earlier poster designs. While after a year's employment he found the factory 'as unbearable as the barracks' in which he had lived during a brief period of military service in 1921, he would nevertheless have learned in this job about the illusion-potentials of wallpaper and how to construct them.[1] This employment was partly necessary because Magritte's father was in financial difficulties owing to a lawsuit against his former partners; but it was also important because he needed to secure an income with which to support Georgette. He states in a letter to Flouquet, noting his inability to produce artistic work:

> If I'm producing nothing it's because I'm not living at the moment. I'm simply loving . . . and as soon as I've secured our material future which is one aim I shall have to find

another to live by and that will be to make Georgette
as happy as possible and in the calm of a nice steady
bourgeois life I shall of course devote myself during my
leisure hours to *the work which I want to leave* after me.[2]

Magritte's later obsession with frames and compartmentalization
was probably influenced by this early experience of working with
wallpaper designs. In another letter of 1921 he notes: 'There's a
special technique to be acquired for this job – small things one
wouldn't suspect, rules to get to know which are well-defined laws
of harmony.'[3] This technique involved the avoidance of showing
movement, and the consideration of flatness – flowers and leaves
should not be superimposed over each other, as this would have
implied a depth inappropriate to wallpaper. As Magritte noted:
'It's absolutely right because in that case there are two planes,
and since wallpaper is decorative the "two dimensions" must be
respected.'[4] His observations on wallpaper design also prefigure the
importance in his future work of repeated images, icons, patterns,
motifs and even titles, and of the tensions that emerged out of the
differences within and between such repetitions. In his paintings
he played with the flatness and two-dimensionality of decorative
patterns, and the characteristic bareness of his colour patches
produces strange contrasts.

Magritte gave up his work at the Peters-Lacroix wallpaper
factory sometime in 1923 and started offering freelance publicity
work to clients in Brussels in 1924. He had already (in 1918) acquired
extensive design experience, beginning with a commission
(probably gained through his father's connections in the stock cube
business) to design a poster advertising Pot au Feu Derbaix (a brand
of beef tea). In early 1924 Magritte urgently needed employment,
and by February he was actively looking for a job in design studios
and interior decorating firms in Paris. After several failed attempts
to find a job or accommodation, he wrote to Georgette: 'It will be

pointless to be separated any longer my dear little wife for if you only know how sad it is for me to go around Paris alone, since the first time I came here was with you!'[5] Magritte's correspondence from this Paris trip suggests discomfort with the Parisian rhythm – a harbinger, perhaps, of his future relationship with the city:

> What I have seen of the bustle of Paris that I have to get used to makes Brussels appear very tranquil and easy-going; in this frame of mind, the greater exhaustion I experienced doing posters in Brussels would seem restful compared to the Parisian bustle. I have seen what is new in the posters here and if I exploited it in Brussels, the effect would be striking . . . I think if you came to Paris, life would be very hard for you, the people here consider themselves superior and despise foreigners . . . everything has greatly changed! Each man for himself, the struggle for life![6]

There is little indication as to whether Magritte came across the budding activities of the French Surrealists, and on this visit he missed by a few months the publication of Breton's first *Surrealist Manifesto* on 15 October 1924.

Later in 1924 Magritte returned to Brussels and secured some commercial work including designing posters for two cinemas (the Coliseum and the Marivaux), commissions for sheet-music cover designs and illustrations for the annual catalogue of the fur house S. Samuel & Cie for which Goemans and Nougé wrote the advertising texts for the 1926 and 1927 publications respectively. Perhaps most importantly, Magritte was commissioned to design for the Brussels couturier Norine, beginning with a full-page colour advertisement (also promoting Alfa Romeo automobiles and the coachbuilders V. Snutsel aîné), which was first published in the November–December 1924 issue of the motoring periodical *Englebert magazine* (Liège).

Norine traded from about 1918 to 1952 under the leadership of Paul-Gustave Van Hecke and his wife Honorine Deschrijver (1887–1977, known as 'Norine'), who defined the style of the fashion house. Magritte was introduced to the couple, probably through Mesens, around 1920. They would both play pivotal roles in supporting Magritte's early career and in more broadly influencing the Belgian art scene during *les années folles* or *dolle jaren*, the post-war period to 1929 when western Europe experienced peace and economic growth. Committed socialists Norine and Van Hecke fostered the Belgian art scene through their couture house and gallery, the latter co-owned with Van Hecke's lifelong business partner André de Ridder. Additional income and promotion came through Van Hecke's literary work as founder of seven cultural journals (including *Variétés*), editor of two socialist newspapers, and as an art and film critic and literary journalist.

Situated at 67 avenue Louise, the Norine premises were directly across from Walter Schwarzenberg's art gallery Le Centaure at number 62, where Magritte would have his first one-man show from 23 April to 3 May 1927. Van Hecke and Schwarzenberg had a mutually useful business relationship – for a percentage on sales Van Hecke secured several of the artists exhibiting at Le Centaure, including Magritte, Frits van den Berghe, Gustave de Smet and Auguste Mambour, each of whom he paid a monthly salary in return for artworks. Magritte yearned for the security of such a guaranteed monthly income throughout his subsequent career, his requests being rebuffed by patrons including the British collector Edward James (in 1938) and later, in the 1950s, his art dealer in America, Alexander Iolas (1907–1987).[7]

Norine also exhibited many artists. Their 1927–8 Autumn/Winter collection viewings were accompanied by an exhibition including works by Magritte, de Smet, Van den Berghe, Max Ernst, Mambour and Floris Jespers. Artists were also commissioned to design invitations and advertisements, with Magritte producing most of the graphic artwork, making the fashion house his most important client at the time. Indeed, the various activities of Van Hecke and Norine, moving between high and popular art and combining painting and fashion design with commercial graphics and advertising, constituted influential contexts for the development of Magritte's own creative versatility. Advertising also offered a significant revenue stream for Magritte after his return from Paris in 1930, following his failed attempt to establish himself there. Unable to support himself through his artistic work, in July 1930 he opened, with Georgette and his brother Paul, the commercial art company Studio Dongo, based in Magritte and Georgette's rented ground-floor apartment at 135 rue Esseghem in Jette, a northwestern suburb of Brussels. Studio Dongo produced a range of posters, advertising and display material for trade fairs and local shop windows.

Magritte's commercial work stretched over a long period, and he continued until 1946 with poster and sheet-music cover design – some of these pieces were signed 'Dongo' or 'Emair' (a phonetic rendering of his reverse initials, M. R.), or with Georgette's maiden name, 'Berger' – along with unsigned studio work. His later posters for film clubs (from 1955 to 1964) and for the Belgian airline Sabena (in 1965) were not produced, as the earlier ones had been, out of necessity, but rather for prestige and other reasons. His commercial and fine art works remained closely interwoven, demonstrating how the emblematic presentation of images characteristic of his poster designs in the 1930s – such as for Boule d'Or cigarettes and a remedy called Inhaléne – can be traced in contemporaneous paintings such as *Summer* from 1931.

Surrealist Beginnings

While Brussels provided some commercial and thus financial relief, Magritte's visits to Paris in the early 1920s in search of similar work were less successful. The city's galleries and exhibitions did, however, provide the opportunity for him to widen his experience of art. He wrote of his first visit to the Louvre, on one of his 1923 Paris trips with Georgette, expressing his awe at the colour of works he had previously seen only in reproductions, in a letter to Lecomte:

> 'The Spring' by Ingres is the finest picture I have seen so far, along with a 'Virgin and child' by Baldovinetti. The 'Greek postures' are presented too theatrically to move me. The 'Mona Lisa' had in front of her an imitation done by one of the too many people who go in for that kind of sport. A few Cézannes, not very important, and Monet who is fairly workmanlike when you see a canvas with its colours.[8]

We can situate the beginnings of Magritte's Surrealist painting in 1925. His engagement with the foremost European avant-garde emerges from his deep involvement in the contexts mapped out so far – the Brussels and wider Belgian modern art scenes, their interactions and exchanges with Parisian movements, and his artistic training and commercial practice. But it also develops out of a key formative context, that of his childhood experiences of the popular cultural life of the place du Manège in Charleroi, an urban space (but non-metropolitan, unlike the bustling and contrasting modernities offered by Brussels and Paris) that exerts a powerful symbolic influence over the development of central elements of Magritte's oeuvre. The place du Manège provided a range of childhood and early youth attractions and experiences that contributed in subtle but clearly detectable ways to the development of his particular style and repertoire of motifs.

This enables us to outline the different, more carnivalesque version of Surrealism that Magritte developed. Indeed, a popular-cultural history of the square and its attractions affords a cultural archaeology of Magritte's art and enables us to see more clearly the roots of his Surrealism – particularly the performative and carnivalesque dimensions expressed in earlier works, many of which have hitherto received scant critical attention.

A major carnivalesque attraction of the place du Manège in the early decades of the twentieth century, and hence during Magritte's early years, was its circus. The square featured a 'cirque permanent',[9] built in 1902 by the Ghent circus architect Auguste Bovyn (it was demolished in 1950 and replaced in 1954 by the Palais des Beaux Arts). Bovyn was celebrated for his innovations in temporary building and tent designs. The permanent circus was the economic engine of its immediate social environment; drawing audiences and making business, it would certainly have been a place frequently visited by Magritte. It attracted many travelling circuses – 'Encore un Cirque!' (Another circus!) exclaims an article from the 16 December 1913 issue of the *Gazette de Charleroi*,[10] announcing the arrival of the circus Hagenbeck (consisting of a menagerie of exotic animals such as lions and leopards).

In April 1913 the Grand Cirque De Jonghe, Belgium's largest circus, founded by Alphonse De Jonghe in 1902, set up its tents in the place du Manège. A newspaper article announced the circus's arrival:

> The special train carrying the equipment, the cavalry and part of the troop arrived this morning at the station of Charleroi (Ville-Haute) . . . The carriages are all luxury, the horses superb. At present, a tent has taken possession of the site . . . the stakes are already buried, and soon the large masts will emerge supporting the giant canvases. The Cirque De Jonghe can hold 3,000 people. Built with the latest refinements of comfort, with easy and safe exits, this immense locale is illuminated with electricity.[11]

Fourteen-year-old Magritte, having been in Charleroi for just
a month, would surely have been excited at witnessing the
construction of this large temporary stage and would have attended
and enjoyed the performances.

The Cirque De Jonghe was famous for its semi-permanent wooden
structure, which not only could accommodate a large number of
visitors but also allowed for spacious performances that would
otherwise be impossible; in particular, equestrian performances were
advertised as major sensations, and a German poster from around
this time reads '40 Horses 40' and 'Mr DE JONGHE performs every
evening at 8pm for his valued audience DRESSAGE PERFORMANCES
unrivalled so far.'[12] Equestrian numbers were a key element of
circuses, as Pierre Bost notes in his book *Le Cirque et le music-hall*
(1931): 'The presentation of a group of horses "at liberty" is one of
the essential attractions for a real circus program. In general, it is
complemented by a "haute école" number [advanced dressage with
a pronounced aerial component].'[13] Of all the potential experiences
offered by the circus to a young viewer, it is these equestrian
performances which seem to have particularly entered into Magritte's
imagery, as we will see later in discussing his *Lost Jockey* paintings.

La Loge

Accommodating into our critical vision the prominence of fairs and
circuses – integral elements of the environments and experiences
of Magritte's childhood and youth – affords new insights into the
significance of likely childhood scenarios and enables explorations
of his works in light of the potential influence on his art of his
experiences of these formative and performative spaces. The circus is
a particular kind of performance space, linked to but different from
the theatre or the concert hall. Magritte's art is deeply concerned
with the representational potentials offered by all such spaces;

René Magritte, *La Loge*, 1925, oil on canvas.

indeed painting itself, contained within the frame as within a kind of stage- or screen-like space, insistently assumes a distinctly theatrical quality in his works, suggesting an abiding preoccupation with the possibilities of understanding art as a kind of performance which involves the presentation of multiple possibilities – of the real, of illusion, of deception and of spectacular or exotic objects, scenes and events. The theatrical space took centre stage early in his work, as can be seen in *La Loge* (The Theatre Box) of 1925.

Magritte's preoccupation with depicting stage-like arenas is part of a wider interest among modernist painters in capturing the spectacle of modern bourgeois society engaged in forms of leisure consumption like attending the theatre. The theme of *La Loge* invites comparison with Pierre-Auguste Renoir's Impressionist paintings of theatregoers, and its title echoes his *La Loge* of 1874, in which Renoir shows two theatregoers in close-up, sitting in a small, cramped cubicle. Framed by red velvet theatrical curtains

Pierre-Auguste Renoir, *La Loge*, 1874, oil on canvas.

and the drapery of the box and its sumptuous colours (their bodies largely engulfed by their lavish clothes), a complex interplay of gazes emerges between these figures, what they are looking at, and the viewer of the painting, who is positioned so that the people depicted become the actors in the theatre taking place within the frame. The male character voyeuristically peeps through his theatre glasses into another box (but pointedly not at the stage below him), unwittingly becoming the object of our gaze; his female companion, looking directly at us, turns us into objects of hers.

Magritte's *La Loge* transforms this claustrophobic place of conflicting gazes into a magnified, empty arena of blank views. Instead of prominent figures publicly displaying their wealth we observe a strange, double-headed female form – like a photographic double-exposure – which disturbingly evokes the spectacular circus displays of conjoined twins. The red lipstick of this figure, who is seated in a relaxed, elongated pose, is reminiscent of that worn by the woman in Renoir's painting, just as the redness of the space Magritte paints echoes the red plush of Renoir's picture, and the female figures in both paintings rest their arms on the seats they sit upon. Magritte evacuates Renoir's claustrophobic space, shifting the theatrical performance from the (undepicted) foreground to a receding background in which we see a girl, her back turned to us, leaning on the frame of what seems to be a viewing ledge, watching whatever performance it contains. Magritte thus merges the theatrical elements suggested by Renoir's painting with elements of modernist perspectival play and suggestions of circus freakshow symbolism to produce a disturbing image of contemporary alienation that, paradoxically, achieves through distance an effect of social claustrophobia similar to that enacted by proximity in Renoir's painting.

Magritte's earliest use of such theatrical staging occurs in 1924 in a painting titled *Woman with a Rose Instead of a Heart*. André Derain's (1880–1954) representations of curtains are an obvious influence on this painting, a significant turning point in Magritte's oeuvre that indicates the beginning of his interest in the theatrical curtain and with it the adoption of staging into his image repertoire. Magritte's writings reveal an ambivalent relation to this artwork. It was important enough for him to mention it in his lecture 'Lifeline 1'. Written in July 1938 and delivered on 20 November 1938 at the Koninklijk Museum voor Schoone Kunsten in Antwerp to an audience of five hundred people, this lecture is one of the most detailed of his rare autobiographical writings. Yet, while he deems the painting important enough to mention, in the same lecture Magritte expresses reservations about it: 'The rose which I put in place of a heart in the bosom of a naked girl did not produce the overwhelming effect I had expected.'[14] Sylvester and Whitfield note that the painting was in Magritte's ownership when he died but that it seems to have previously been owned by his friend and first art dealer, Paul-Gustave Van Hecke.[15] Perhaps the ambivalence lay less in the failed attempt to represent objects than in the budding realization of the importance of this early representation of the stage scenario which threads throughout his oeuvre. The familiar elements of curtain, table, window/screen/painting and enclosed room are all already present here, and in many subsequent images they combine to produce Magritte's haunting scenes of the alienation found in the most private and intimate place, the bourgeois home. Indeed, Magritte refined the eroticized and intimate atmosphere of *Woman with a Rose Instead of a Heart* into repeated representations of his own home, insistently positioning the viewer as gazing illicitly onto a secretive scene.

René Magritte,
*Woman with a Rose
Instead of a Heart*,
1924, oil on canvas.

The circus offers a particular variety of theatrical space that becomes a key part of Magritte's stagings. *Perpetual Motion* (1935) depicts a circus weightlifter clad in leopard-skin vest, raising a barbell with his left hand so that the right-hand ball obscures his face, which nevertheless appears, ghost-like, on the surface of the ball, in a visual pun.[16] In the background stand assorted solid geometric forms and a wooden barrel, reflected in the glassy water of a pond amid a grassy landscape that stretches back to distant mountains. The painting exploits circus imagery to achieve Magritte's characteristic mysterious effect – identity, sculptural stasis and the doubling of reflections construct a complex allegory of the movements of difference between the balanced balls of the barbell, the objects and their reflections, the arrangement of figure and objects against the (literal) field of the image, all subsumed under the superficially enigmatic title.

The Lost Jockey

We can trace the development of this kind of circus imagery clearly in Magritte's equestrian paintings, starting with his 1926 *The Lost Jockey* and continuing in later works such as *The Endless Chain* (1938) and *The Blank Cheque* (1965). These paintings draw on the equestrian traditions associated with circus acts and seem to allude in particular to the performances of dressage. *The Endless Chain* was painted in February 1938 and (according to Magritte's letter to the British collector Edward James from 22 September 1937) tries to resolve what he calls 'problems' – in this case, the problem of the horse. In a later letter from 27 December of the same year this preoccupation continues: 'I am still trying to solve "the problem of the horse" and so far have found only unconvincing solutions or poetic solutions.'[17] He relates one such poetic solution:

In a dark room, a horsewoman sitting near a table and resting her head on one hand is looking at a horse entirely covered by a country landscape (as if the top part of the horse were the same colour as the sky and the lower part, from the line of the horizon downwards, had the appearance of fields and a road).[18]

Magritte narrates the actual solution again in a later, prank letter dated 3 February 1938 that he dictated to Edith de Vuyst at the Palais des Beaux-Arts in Brussels and sent under her signature to Marcel Mariën, presenting it as the explanation for a riddle or a magic trick:

Dear Sir, I have just seen René Magritte who has given me all the necessary information about 'the problem of the horse' with which you are rightly preoccupied.

The matter having been fully clarified for me, I will give you the solution.

The horse is indeed the nub of the whole business but is mounted not by a single rider but by three, all most elegantly dressed: History represented at its most illustrious epochs.

Here first near the mane: Antiquity with its short tunic and small, curly-haired head, then the gallant musketeer all top-boots and plumed hat, and last in time but uniquely distinguished our Modern horseman in his bowler-hat and ample tie.[19]

The three men sitting on the horse recall the popular generic dressage poses and acts employing multiple riders on a single horse used in many circuses. It can also be found in early twentieth-century postcard advertisements for the Cirque De Jonghe act 'Les 4 de Jonghe Equestrians', where the riders comprise two generations of De Jonghe family members.

The first of Magritte's equestrian paintings is *The Lost Jockey*. Painted in 1926, it reappears in many versions throughout

René Magritte, *The Lost Jockey*, 1926, oil on canvas.

his oeuvre and seems in consequence to embody a series of significances to do with artistic repetition and mechanical reproduction. According to Sylvester and Whitfield it was the first image Magritte repeated – a practice that would become a significant trait, or what Nathalia Brodskaïa calls (with a more commercial overtone) a 'trademark', in his work.[20] This painting also marks a particularly formative moment (or perhaps a repetition of moments) in his artistic development, as he comments in his 1954 'Autobiographical Sketch' (referring to himself in the third person):

> He executed the painting 'The Lost Jockey', conceived with no aesthetic intention, with the sole aim of RESPONDING to a mysterious feeling, a 'causeless' anguish, a sort of 'call to order'

which impinged on his consciousness at certain non-historic moments and which had guided his life ever since birth.[21]

In an interview with Jacques Goossens in 1966, a year before Magritte's death, he emphasized the importance of *The Lost Jockey* in relation to another sequence of formative artistic moments:

Goossens: One day Marcel Lecomte showed you one of de Chirico's works?

Magritte: Ah yes, the encounter here really was more significant than with the Futurists, because the Futurists were working on a new way of painting, whereas de Chirico was not concerned with a way of painting but with *what must be painted*, which is quite a different thing . . . It was *Le Chant d'amour*, actually, a very beautiful picture . . .

Goossens: And then I believe you set about painting with all your might at that point?

Magritte: Ah, I painted . . . yes . . . but . . . I couldn't paint like de Chirico – or rather Kirico – I was searching for something to paint, you see, like de Chirico, and I couldn't paint what de Chirico painted . . . Yes, it was my first exhibition [at Le Centaure] which really represented what I consider to be worthwhile in my . . . in my work . . . Yes, [*The Lost Jockey*] was the first canvas I truly painted, feeling I had found my way, if I can use this term.[22]

The Lost Jockey was not only the first of his pictures that Magritte 'considered worthwhile', it was also the first of his paintings to be reproduced, in an article published by Camille Goemans in September 1926.[23] Goemans identified Magritte himself as the subject of this painting, describing it as 'René Magritte hurtling recklessly into the void'.[24] In the March 1927 issue of the Brussels-based art journal *Sélection*, Paul-Gustave Van Hecke, its co-founder and Magritte's art dealer at the time, published the first article to focus exclusively on Magritte, describing him as 'the jockey who lost his way'.[25] This triple significance (first 'worthwhile' picture; first motif to be repeated; first to be reproduced in a journal) suggests an element of persistence of vision in Magritte's use, in different versions of *The Lost Jockey*, of insistently repetitive imagery deriving from childhood experiences.

The image of the cantering horseman has, in consequence, entered the history and mythology surrounding Magritte's life and oeuvre and is used by critics to mark decisive points in his development as an artist. Many critics follow Goemans in reading the jockey as a representation of Magritte himself. The importance of 'the jockey who lost his way' is evident in Mariën's selection of the 1943 version as the first plate in his monograph of that year, the first on Magritte's work. These narratives around *The Lost Jockey* have themselves established the critical convention that the painting is now identified as Magritte's first Surrealist work. Brodskaïa describes it as a 'truly prophetic painting', asserting that 'Magritte regarded *The Lost Jockey*, painted in 1926, as his first Surrealist painting.'[26]

The painting's significance in biographical narratives of Magritte's oeuvre has tended to overshadow critical analyses of its actual content and possible meanings, as well as its relations to artistic traditions. Sylvester points to Paolo Uccello's *The Hunt in the Forest* (*c.* 1468) as a possible source, noting that Uccello was the Surrealists' preferred Old Master and the only one mentioned in the first *Surrealist Manifesto* in 1924 as a Surrealist *avant la lettre*.[27] According to Charles Alexandre, Magritte too had, during his student days at the Academy around 1917/18, a particular interest in Uccello and his contemporaries. With the Academy's infrequent openings, and galleries and museums stripped during the German occupation, Magritte would have most likely seen Uccello's work in reproduction. We can glean another visual source of the jockey from the observation of the Antwerp-born, New York-based lawyer Harry Torczyner, one of Magritte's most important collectors and supporters after their first meeting in 1957, who noted that the jockey might derive from Magritte's apparent habit in the 1920s of visiting racecourses.[28]

The jockey can also be traced back to Magritte's extensive use of the illustrations accompanying entries in charts for *cheval* (horse) and *équitation* (equestrianism) in the popular *Larousse* encyclopaedias, which were often advertised as household essentials in early twentieth-century national and regional Belgian newspapers.[29] *Larousse* encyclopaedias also provided the source images for Max Ernst's jockeys in *Dada Degas* (1920–21). Magritte was very familiar with Ernst's work and it clearly influenced his own development. Throughout Magritte's oeuvre, we find enlarged painterly reproductions of a variety of illustrations from different versions of *Larousse*.[30] According to Sylvester's notes on Magritte's library, he owned at the time of his death volumes I and II of *Larousse: Universelle* (1922–3) and volumes I and II of Larousse's *L'Art des origines à nos jours* (Art from its Origins to the Present Day, 1932). Indeed, leafing through the different volumes of *Larousse* is at times like rummaging through Magritte's box of props: for example, the stormy seascape with a capsizing boat of *The Difficult Crossing* (painted in 1926, the same year as the first *The Lost Jockey*) originates in the *Larousse* entry on 'Le Naufrage, d'après J. Vernet' (The Shipwreck, after J. Vernet). In *The Learned Tree* of 1935, a tree's bark opens like cabinet doors to reveal objects lodged within – this 'cabinet of curiosities' appears in *Larousse* under the rubric of *récolte du liège* (cork harvest), showing men removing the bark from a tree to make corks for wine bottles.[31] *Larousse* constitutes a major resource that clearly stimulates key elements of Magritte's developing dialogue with Surrealism. The origins of the images for *The Lost Jockey* in his encounters with Renaissance pictorialism and in contemporary popular encyclopaedia illustrations indicate the range of cultural sources from which Magritte's particular brand of Surrealism was developing in the 1920s.

But the sources for this important painting extend beyond pictorial ones to include elements and influences drawn from the fairground and circus environments experienced by the young Magritte. A quarter of the right-hand side of the 1926 painting is obscured by a red curtain, partly drawn back to reveal the scene depicted, a theatrical cue reminiscent of *La Loge*, inviting the viewer into a performative space containing the circus-ring-like area across which the jockey seems to be moving. Together with the horseman, this curtain evokes typical poster advertisements for circus performances featuring *manèges* (riding schools) framed by red curtains and showing dressage acts. In *The Lost Jockey*, the floor's dark colour and geometrically patterned composition are reminiscent of the structures of the circus ring, and elegantly carved poles seem to support the branches of trees, reversing the sequence of human/mechanical intervention that transforms the living tree into ornamental turned wood. Magritte called these poles *bilboquets* (also the title of a 1923 pamphlet by Antonin Artaud, translated in the Calder edition as the children's toy 'cup and ball'), and they occur frequently throughout his oeuvre. Deriving from a *Larousse* illustration, his earliest use of the *bilboquet* motif is in one of his first 'Surrealist' paintings, *Cinéma bleu* (1925; discussed below), again affirming the significance of Larousse for Magritte's stylistic development. In *The Lost Jockey* these *bilboquets* combine with the other imagery in the painting to connote a circus. They clearly resemble tent poles in an arena, while their strange organic branchings recall the rods and ropes used to hold up a tent.

Magritte's riffing on the circus is clearer still in a *papier collé*, gouache and ink on paper version of *The Lost Jockey*, also from

René Magritte, *The Lost Jockey*, 1926, *papier collé,* gouache and ink on paper.

1926. Here the scene is framed on both sides by dark curtains. The floor's geometric patterning (a recurring feature in his paintings of 1925–6) again resembles the flattened-out folds of a circus tent ceiling and its awnings, and evokes the 'omnitriangulated' surface characteristic of a geodesic dome – a pattern Magritte used in many of his *papiers collés* at the time. The geodesic dome is an iconic architectural structure of modernity, associated with the work of Richard Buckminster Fuller (1895–1983). The first such dome was constructed by the firm of Dyckerhoff & Widmann on the roof of the Zeiss optics plant in Jena, Germany, and a larger dome, the Zeiss-Planetarium, called 'The Wonder of Jena', opened to the public on 18 July 1926 – it is possible, then, that Magritte saw the design in press photographs of the time reporting this opening.

With its structural resemblance to a carousel this *papier collé* of *The Lost Jockey* marries associations of the circus with those of the fairground – the horse and rider, poles and ornately patterned background propelling the viewer back to the 1913 scene of the place du Manège and its turning carousel. The modern carousel emerged from early jousting traditions in Europe and the Middle East, where knights galloped in a circle while tossing balls to each other, with the first fairground carousels emerging in the early eighteenth century. Philippe Dimbourg, in his book on Belgian fairs, illustrates the Charleroi ones with two images of early twentieth-century carousels, demonstrating their significance but also their typical themes at the time of Magritte's youth.[32] It is of course possible that the carousel in one of Dimbourg's illustrations may even depict the one on which Georgette and Magritte met. The illustration shows rows of four galloping, white wooden horses interspersed with gondola-style compartments. Facing to the right and rotating counterclockwise, they moved up and down via a rotating ceiling called an *ascenseur* (elevator). Dimbourg notes that the theme of the carousel in Charleroi (in keeping with the connotations of *manège* as a circular arena in which to train horses) was based on an equestrian act in a circus where the

Charleroi fair carousel, early 20th century.

'delicately "baroque" decorations' of the ceiling and its turned poles resembled the structure of a circus tent.[33]

Viewed in relation to this image and its contexts, the light-brown floor of Magritte's *papier collé* suggests both the sawdust of the circus floor and the wooden flooring of a carousel. The lost jockey in this structure does not 'hurtle towards a void' – which would imply a linear movement in one direction – but instead becomes part of the circular, repetitive course of a carousel horse rotating to looped circus music. The *bilboquets*, still reminiscent of tent poles but now bearing leafless, antler-like tree branches, are here composed not of wood but of fragments of sheet music, alluding both to the circular, repetitive tunes played as a carousel rotates and to the important role of music accompanying circus performances (and to Magritte's work illustrating sheet music). Pierre Bost notes of an equestrian performance, 'if it were presented to us without music, it would not touch us', linking this 'touching' the audience to the 'naive need to believe that the horse dances, even if we know it does not'.[34]

The music fragments in Magritte's *papier collé* can clearly be decoded; they derive from a popular but now largely forgotten British musical play from Magritte's childhood called *The Girls of Gottenburg*, written in 1907 by George Grossmith Junior (co-author with his brother Weedon, in 1892, of the popular comic novel *The Diary of a Nobody*). The music of the play is by Ivan Caryll and Lionel Monckton, and the words in the passage chosen by Magritte and used for the *bilboquet* on the left read 'Sprechen Sie Deutsch, mein Herr?' ('Do you speak German, Sir?', spoken by the character Mitzi, the innkeeper's daughter), while the middle *bilboquet* of the five, placed to the right of centre, contains fragments of a dialogue: Mitzi sings, 'And in the afternoons . . . ', and Otto, Prince of Saxe-Hildesheim, played in the original performance by Grossmith himself, completes her sentence, 'You walk on the sands, and listen to bands.' In the play (but not included in Magritte's

picture), Mitzi's next line reads: 'Perhaps you travel to Margate.'[35]
Apart from the obvious echo of Magritte's name, the mention of
Margate perhaps suggests that Magritte is alluding by connotative
extension to T. S. Eliot's 1922 poem *The Waste Land* (a controversial
and widely read work of high modernism), which contains the
lines 'on Margate sands./ I can connect/ Nothing with nothing'
and which mixes English music-hall traditions with classical and
literary references to produce a complex polysemic poem. Clearly
alluding to the English music-hall tradition, the music Magritte has
incorporated into the *papier collé* also evokes the kind of music that
would have been played on fairground rides.

Magritte's *papier collé* in its entirety performs a kind of dynamic
condensation into a series of key elements – horse and rider (from
Larousse), poles and supported fabric tent, wooden floors and visual
evocations of context-appropriate music from an early twentieth-
century theatrical text – of the multisensory popular-cultural
experience of the circus/fairground attractions of his childhood
and youth. Its complex merging of autobiographical elements with
implications of and allusions to wider cultural contexts indicates
again Magritte's ability to combine elements from a wide variety
of sources into a single and singular, symbolically evocative image
which nevertheless constitutes a key element in a sequence of
similar images that relate to each other as extended variations on
recurrent themes. In these works Magritte generates a nuanced and
carefully structured exploration of the multi-layered intersections
and interdependencies of elements of high and popular modernist
cultures with conscious and unconscious dimensions of personal
memory and experience. In doing so he is also subtly redirecting
French Surrealism's exploration of the relations between aesthetic
creation and the forces of unconscious desires and urges towards the
specifically Belgian positions outlined in the debates and disputes
noted earlier – particularly in regard to such areas of disagreement
as the relation between Breton's 'auditive' and 'visual' images (which,

Magritte's works imply, is rather more complex and less hierarchical than Breton would have it), and the related resistance of the Belgian Surrealists to Bretonian ideas about the primacy of automatic creativity as a mode of Surrealist aesthetic production.

Resituating these early *Lost Jockey* pictures in relation to the childhood contexts of circuses and fairgrounds suggested by Magritte's own autobiographical narratives enables us to align them with previous artistic traditions representing the hustle and bustle of popular amusement venues. Specifically we might note their resemblance to Henri de Toulouse-Lautrec's paintings of circuses and other popular amusement venues in Paris. Described in an article of 4 June 1914 in the Belgian social democratic newspaper *Le Peuple* as a 'peintre prolétarien' (a painter of the underclass),[36] Toulouse-Lautrec (1864–1901) was a well-recognized and appreciated artist in Belgium. Magritte would have been familiar with his work, as Toulouse-Lautrec was well established in Belgian art circles by the turn of the century, being exhibited in Brussels in the 1888 and 1890 annual exhibitions of Les xx, a Brussels-based group of twenty Belgian sculptors, designers and painters that also included one of Magritte's favourites, James Ensor (1860–1949). Les xx was formed in 1883 in response to the rejection of Ensor's *The Oyster Eater* for the 1883 salon of the avant-gardist L'Essor group. The annual exhibitions of Les xx included works by twenty invited international artists, among them the French painters Camille Pissarro (1880–1903), Claude Monet (1840–1926) and Paul Cézanne (1839–1906), and the Dutchman Vincent van Gogh (1853–1890).

Brussels hosted one of Toulouse-Lautrec's first exhibitions, and certainly his first international one, as in 1888 Les xx and 'L'exposition international d'affiches' exhibited two of his circus drawings, including his famous 1887/8 *Equestrienne (At the Cirque Fernando)*. Cirque Fernando was established by the acrobat and equestrian Fernando in the boulevard de Rochechouart in Paris, between the rue des Martyrs and the present rue Viollet-le-Duc, and opened on 25 June 1875. Its proximity to Montmartre meant it was frequented by – and influenced the work of – many artists, including Renoir (who painted *Acrobats at the Cirque Fernando* in 1879), Seurat (whose last, unfinished painting, *Le cirque* of 1890–91, depicted a female rider standing on her horse in the ring of the Cirque Fernando) and Degas (who painted *Miss La-La at the Cirque Fernando* in 1879). Cirque Fernando went through a number of successful ownerships, eventually transforming into the Cirque Medrano when the clown Géronimo Medrano took over in 1890. It remained for some time a favourite place for artists and by 1928 (now under the ownership of Géronimo's son Jérôme) had become a hub of the Parisian entertainment scene at which the most successful circus acts performed. This period of public prominence coincides with René and Georgette Magritte living in Paris from September 1927 to the end of 1930. As part of the vibrant artistic scene around Montmartre, they would have visited it as well as its competitor, the Cirque d'Hiver at 110 rue Amelot (at the junction with rue des Filles Calvaires) in the eleventh arrondissement. Cirque Medrano's advertising often featured equestrian acts – a particularly frequently used image depicted a female rider on a galloping horse, evoking the partially invisible, enforested female jockey and horse shown in Magritte's later work *The Blank Cheque* from 1965. The historical connection between Toulouse-Lautrec visiting Cirque Fernando and Magritte visiting Cirque Medrano establishes an interesting link between the two artists.

Toulouse-Lautrec's subsequent exhibitions in Belgium in the late nineteenth and early twentieth century, such as the international ix Salon de la Libre Esthétique in 1902, received overwhelmingly positive responses, as indicated by a review published on 1 February 1894: 'The success went naturally to the Parisians, to Chèret, and to Besnard's incomparable palette, and to Toulouse-Lautrec.'[37] Magritte may also have seen publications

Henri de Toulouse-Lautrec, *At the Circus: Jockey*, 1899, graphite, black and coloured pastel and charcoal on off-white heavy wove paper.

that included reproductions of Toulouse-Lautrec's works: 22 of his circus drawings were published in 1905 by Libraire de France in the volume *Au cirque* and, more interestingly still, the French Flammarion published in 1926 (thus coinciding with the first *The Lost Jockey* works) an extensive volume entitled *Le Théâtre, le cirque et le music-hall et les peintres du XVIIIe siècle à nos jours*, which included reproductions of works by Toulouse-Lautrec, Renoir, Degas and Seurat.

Magritte's lost jockeys evoke the rider and the rounded structures of the circus ring in Toulouse-Lautrec's *At the Circus: Jockey* of 1899. In Toulouse-Lautrec's drawing the jockey sits backwards, mounted bareback on a cantering horse's rump, giving it the whip just as Magritte's jockey does – albeit facing front and in a saddle – while driving his horse through the forest of *bilboquets*. The minimal background detail in Toulouse-Lautrec's drawing creates a sense of daredevilry, of freedom and space within the confinement of the circus ring, contrasting with Magritte's rather more crowded image in which the jockey's freedom is constricted by the curtains (suggestive again of bourgeois domestic/theatrical stuffiness). Both pictures allude to the circularity and repetition associated with the circus and the carousel; both evoke in different ways Eadweard Muybridge's stop-motion photographic frames of a galloping horse that formed, in 1878, one of the earliest moving pictures. Both pieces exploit an implicit tension between the simultaneous human restraint and vulnerability of the rider, and the freedom of natural movement associated with a cantering horse.

3

Going to the Pictures

It is difficult to overestimate the importance to Magritte's art of
the cinematic space, and of film projection: the combination of
moving images with their comical, illusory and deceptive effects,
and (during the age of silent film) their musical accompaniment.
The cinema offered a specific kind of theatrical space in which
traditional modes of public and shared experience and perception
merged with fast-moving technological innovation. Cinema-
going would be a lifelong passion for Magritte, and cinematic
experience and effects are a continuous concern in and influence
on the ideas in his art. Art historian Robert Short summarizes
some of the rhetorical dimensions of cinema's influence on
Magritte, enumerating his development of pictorial equivalents
to filmic devices such as montage, framing, point of view,
camera movement, simultaneity, depth of field and narrative
sequentiality.[1]

Michel Draguet, in his biography of Magritte, describes
the cinema as a 'lieu magique', a magical place, and, like the
fairground and the circus, the cinema also offered transitory
experiences of leisure and pleasure, of excitement and
carnivalesque escape from the tedium of daily bourgeois life.[2]
Cinemas and other scopic performances and displays were
indeed significant elements of the entertainment repertoires
of fairs. While itinerant photographers were a familiar
attraction from the 1840s on, Guido Convents notes that

from the moment that moving picture apparatus and films came on the market, they were almost immediately picked up by showmen who worked the fairs. Roughly estimated, it can be said that between 1896 and 1914 about fifty (probably more) showmen regularly brought moving pictures to Belgian fairs.[3]

These travelling cinemas showed films by Georges Méliès and the Lumière brothers alongside Pathé productions – for example Willem Fortuin's company, taking over from Henri Grünkorn, showed the latest films across Belgium, such as Méliès' *Le Voyage dans la lune* (Trip to the Moon) in 1904. Cinema audiences often comprised schoolchildren enticed by special 'educational' discounts offered either to beat competitors or to pacify local authorities. As a schoolboy, Magritte would have frequented many such screenings. More significantly still, in 1908 a glut of travelling shows in Belgian cities meant that many showmen travelled instead to the villages and smaller towns, including Lessines, in search of new locales and audiences.

If, in 1925, Magritte's *La Loge* already introduces several key tropes – the darkened space of projection or performance, the figure of a viewer, the theatrical stage and the cinematic screen – as important elements in Magritte's stylistic and formal repertoire, his *Cinéma bleu*, painted in the same year, makes this significance explicit and anchors it firmly to his time in Charleroi, in close proximity to the place du Manège. *Cinéma bleu* is a painterly collage literally presenting a series of different stages. Heavy theatre or cinema stage curtains frame a De Chirico-esque Greek building, a temple which is itself a space of performance (perhaps connoting the cinema as a kind of modern temple). Other elements in the painting include a posed female figure, possibly taken from an advertising image (and used again by Magritte in 1926 for a sheet-music cover illustration), a hot-air balloon flying in the distance and a prototype of the recurring *bilboquet*. The front of

René Magritte, *Cinéma bleu*, 1925, oil on canvas.

the stage features a sign stating 'CINÉMA BLEU' beneath an arrow pointing off to the right. Art historian Haim Finkelstein argues that this painting foreshadows central themes in Magritte's future work, which, he suggests, centre on a 'systematic disruption of Renaissance space'.[4] He connects Magritte's painting with the frontal, layered conception and flattening of space of Max Ernst's collages, arguing that the 'illusionist representation of layers' in *Cinéma bleu* and 'the spatial ambiguities and paradoxes' emerging out of it are directly influenced by cinema.[5] The arrow in the painting literally points to the cinematic image as a major future path of Magritte's artistic work.

Irène Hamoir writes in her 'Notes biographiques' on Magritte that the title of *Cinéma bleu* related to a specific cinema in Charleroi – apparently one of the few things Magritte remembered from his teenage years there. Born only two years after the invention of cinematic projection in 1895, and just as the first film studios were being built, Magritte's early life coincides with the development of the film industry and its rapid establishment as a primary form of mass entertainment. By the start of the First World War there were over six hundred movie theatres across Belgium, with Pathé (then one of the biggest film producers in Europe) establishing Le Belge Cinéma, a distribution company, in Brussels in 1908. Convents notes that 'in about two or three years [Pathé] had a cinema hall in almost every Belgian city which screened a quality programme once or twice a week, delivered from the Brussels Pathé headquarters.'[6] The *Gazette de Charleroi* reported on 24 October 1912 that the city had record numbers of cinemas that year.[7] Cinema's popularity and ubiquity (but also its dangers as a potential tool of miseducation of the masses) are clear from another article on 1 April 1912:

Cinemas multiply in the conurbation in an unheard-of way . . . The cinema often doubles as a brewery . . . In every suburb as well as in the capital, this multiplication of cinemas requires very great precautions to avoid any danger of fire. Perhaps the most serious danger is the deprivation of childhood . . .

In general, the cinema should be less dependent on the scenarios of soap operas, which are merely grand diversions for concierges. It must be refined, but if it refines itself too much, will the mass obey the same enthusiasm?[8]

Probably around the time of the family's move to Charleroi, Magritte's father bought him a Pathé camera, with which Magritte made short films. The Cinéma Bleu, which opened in 1911 in Charleroi's rue Neuve, one street up from the place du Manège, was a short distance from his home address. Its walls were apparently entirely painted in blue, perhaps making the venue an originary version of the sky-blue enclosed box we recognize in various manifestations in Magritte's works. With his brother Paul working there as a ticket salesman, Magritte had the possibility of visiting film showings whenever he wanted.

Cinema-going was, at the time, a largely unregulated and potentially dangerous affair. Overcrowding, projector fires, unrestricted public smoking and other potential hazards led to catastrophes across the modern world that were enthusiastically covered by the sensationalist Belgian press, constituting a constant narrative of international public disasters with which the young Magritte would have been familiar. The *Gazette de Charleroi* carried many reports on several local and international cinema-related accidents. On 31 December 1911 it reported on both the burning down of a cinema in Bologoye, Russia, in which ninety people died, and a bomb attack on the Wintergarten cinema in Liège earlier the same month.[9] On 3 March 1912 we read of a film operator in Madrid being killed by an electric spark, which in turn caused a panic in which a number of people were injured; on 29 May that year the paper reported on cinema fires killing and injuring people in the Castellón province of Villarreal; and many people were killed in the ensuing panic after an explosion in a New York cinema, as covered in the 4 February 1913 edition.[10] The prevailing moral climate in Belgium also found cinemas and moving pictures to be potentially dangerous, and many perceived psychological and moral concerns developed in relation to cinema. A *Gazette de Charleroi* report of 23 February 1913 describes the concerns raised by an Italian neurologist that the vibratory movements of the film can be unfavourable for neurasthenics and, more gravely still, for children with nervous conditions, while the darkness of the auditorium, described as taking on 'the appearance of the marvellous and occult', might intensify to a dangerous level young people's experience of cinematographic projection.[11] This description perhaps explains Magritte's early fascination with cinema, and prefigures the significance of cinema for Surrealism and its quest for the marvellous.

Films introduced audiences to the whole world, from the exotic to the most familiar locations. In 1912–13 in Charleroi the cinema programmes featured a huge variety of film genres, ranging from heart-wrenching dramas of intimacy such as *La Dame aux camélias* (a silent adaptation of the play by Alexandre Dumas, starring Sarah Bernhardt and directed by André Calmettes, Louis Mercaton and Henri Pouctal), which showed at the Cinéma de la Montagne in March 1912, to documentaries presenting 'vues du Far-West, de la prairie et des pampas' (views of the far West, the prairie and the pampas);[12] from hilarious Pathé slapstick movies and comedies like the *Rigadin* films (which starred actors like Stacia Napierkowska, Max Linder and his rival Charles Prince, the latter two both playing upper-class dandies constantly in trouble with authority figures and embroiled in complex love interests), to educational programmes about overseas cities and cultures. The latest news programmes were assembled by the Pathé brothers and presented as the *Pathé Journal*, with family (edited) matinées starting at 2 p.m., and soirées with unedited presentations of the events of the week shown at 8 p.m. The *Journal* demonstrates cinema's unparalleled ability to provide unprecedentedly up-to-date information to mass audiences (for example, footage was shown in late April 1912 of the sinking of the *Titanic*, only a couple of weeks after the disaster). A budding artist like Magritte would have been profoundly susceptible to the powerful visual influence of the cinema.

The First World War and the German invasion of neutral Belgium in August 1914 dramatically reduced the number of films available and required an increasing part of each cinema's programme to be given over to war reportage. Paradoxically, such rationing and genre-restriction may have had the effect of intensifying the audience's experience. During the war the Belgian army held on to a small part of the coastline known as 'Free Belgium', which remained under the rule of King Albert I and his exiled Belgian government. Here cinemas continued to show an uncensored selection of films. The rest of the country was occupied by the harsh German Imperial Army, which committed numerous war crimes including massacres, mass executions and deliberate urban destruction, during what has come to be known as the Rape of Belgium. Brussels surrendered meekly to Germany on 20 August 1914, and the occupying army quickly introduced curfews, identity cards and press censorship. The Flemish language and Flemish administration were enforced (Magritte and his family were French speakers), and clocks were put forward an hour to adopt German time.

The cityscape Magritte experienced in Brussels after his move there in November 1915 differed dramatically from the pre-war one. The effects of war transformed urban space in surreal ways – food shortages meant that parks and green spaces were requisitioned for vegetable production, and temporary hospitals were erected in halls and even in the grounds of the King's Palace. The German army requisitioned anything helpful for the war effort: rubber, wool, copper, cars, horses, bicycles, even the pigeons used by the Belgians as message carriers – all were suddenly invested with new value because of their military significance. The Monument au Pigeon-Soldat, erected in 1930 in the park off the rue Locquenghien, commemorates the roles played by messenger pigeons in the war. The regular appearance of these birds – and of doves in particular – in Magritte's later paintings suggests a persistent memory of their sudden importance during this period.

Occupied Belgium differed significantly from the Belgium of the pre-war years, and cinema-going did not escape the pervasive influence of new, oppressive regulations. Film historian Leen Engelen discusses some of the transformations of the cinema experience under German rule:

> Theater owners were not only subject to different legislations, they also depended on different film distribution networks and consequently on different films, different film stars and different audiences. Moreover, movie theaters for the troops were established on both sides of the frontline: in the German *Etappengebiet*, they were called 'War Cinemas' (*Kriegs-Kino*) or 'Field Cinemas' (*Feldkino*) and were operated by the Imperial Army. On the allied side, they were usually referred to as *cinémas de l'armée* or 'front cinemas' and were supervised by the Belgian or British military . . . [or] by local entrepreneurs or charity organisations like the YMCA.[13]

These rigid divisions along linguistic, nationalist and occupied/free lines temporarily exposed and exploited ideological faults in the Belgian national consciousness (divided into Flemish and Walloon cultures, Flemish- and French-speaking communities which mingled and coexisted quite comfortably during peacetime) that otherwise remained latent, and may have influenced in subtle ways Magritte's lifelong painterly explorations and deconstructions of divisions and oppositions. Many cinemas closed down in late 1914 during the first chaotic months of the occupation, and, as Engelen notes, Germany's censorship laws clamped down on

> almost all media distributed in Belgium, such as texts, pictures, sheet music, theatre plays, newspapers, and . . . film. It was decreed that any communication or work of art not explicitly authorized was implicitly banned. Consequently, every film had to be evaluated by the German censors before appearing on screen.[14]

These new regulations dramatically restricted imports of new films; however 'all pre-war allied productions submitted to the censors before mid-May 1915 were still accepted', and by this time most cinemas were returning to business and were able to run repeat showings of many older films.[15]

Cinéma Bleu's wartime programmes indicate the impact of the occupation on film-going. While it is difficult to trace their original showings during Magritte's stay in Charleroi, the rescreenings shown during the war give us an idea about which films Cinéma Bleu owned and therefore would have shown regularly in this period. In October 1915 the Cinéma Bleu reopened – perhaps following a temporary closure brought about by the start of the war. It often rescreened pre-war films, including the Italian *Quo Vadis* (dir. Enrico Guazzoni, 1913; considered by many to be the first feature film due to its two-hour running time); *La Tour de l'expiation* (The Tower of Terror), a 1913 Italian film directed by Roberto Roberti; and Magritte's favourites – Victorin-Hippolyte Jasset's very successful film series starring Pierre Bressol, produced for the company Éclair and based on two characters from American popular fiction, Nick Carter and Nat Pinkerton (Jasset made *Zigomar contre Nick Carter* in 1912). The significance of these characters in Belgian popular culture at the time of the First World

War is clear from the adverts promoting these rescreenings. One from 7 November 1915 describes the 'great applause' of the crowd in response to a screening of the 1912 Nat Pinkerton movie *Le Vol de la malle des Indes* (The Theft of the Indian Trunk), 'guaranteeing full-house' at the Cinéma Bleu for the showings.[16] On 30 October 1915 Cinéma Bleu rescreened two Pinkerton films, Jasset's *Le Mirage* (1912) and *Le Phare tragique* (1912).[17] Many other cinemas across Belgium showed Pinkerton films: the 'splendid programme' of the Théâtre Varia in Jumet (now part of Charleroi) included *Nat Pinkerton contre Tous* (1912) in July 1916;[18] the 1911 film *L'Auberge sanglante* (The Bloody Hostel), shown together with four other Pinkerton films;[19] and *Les Pilleurs de musées* (1913) was shown in December 1915 at the Cinéma du Progrès in a wider non-cinematic programme including variety performances of comic acrobats, indicating that cinematic spaces were also able and willing during this period to accommodate older forms of carnivalesque public entertainment to supplement their depleted film reserves.[20]

It is likely that the young Magritte, who as noted earlier had moved to Brussels in 1915, would have frequented the cinemas of the capital and watched (probably repeatedly) many of these movies, which he would have already seen at the Cinéma Bleu, providing a potential repertoire of innovative rhetorical devices and (through the familiarity built by repeated viewings) a huge and formative image bank of visual material for the trainee artist. His particular interest in the American detective character Nat Pinkerton, which originated in rewatching the movies of this period, is clear from his own brief narrative (published in *La Carte d'après nature* in April 1953) based around this detective. Magritte's 'Nat Pinkerton' offers a condensed parody of the detective narrative and its structure. In short, simple sentences, the tale presents a typical day in the life of the detective, starting with his arrival in his office in the morning, and relates various humdrum events in the typical working day, culminating in an evening visit to 'a quiet café to play a game of piquet before going home', where 'he is busy writing a play with his wife and mother-in-law, who are actresses.'[21] Its deadpan, simple realist style lacks romantic excitement, incredible action, coincidences, plot twists or sudden revelations – in short, it is as different from a conventional detective narrative as it is possible to be, a stripping-down of the genre to the bare elements of pure fictional convention (paradoxically affirming Fredric Jameson's insight about detective fiction that 'readers just thought they cared about nothing but the action; that really, although they didn't know it, the thing they cared about, and that I cared about, was the creation of emotion through dialogue and description'[22]).

In effect, Magritte's pseudo-detective narrative constitutes his declaration of independence from the kinds of narrative trickery associated with the will-to-know characteristic of detective fiction. This latter he implicitly associates with the trickery of Bretonian Surrealism, in which the unconscious is used to figure a knowable mystery that will reveal itself through the productions of automatic writing and similar practices. In an act of Surrealist subversion, Magritte celebrates instead the utter banality of Nat Pinkerton's life, excising from it any notion of the marvellous or, indeed, the unconscious of dream and desire (although Magritte's Pinkerton has the ambition to write) and leaving only surface events, habits and simple, repeated actions. Many critics, and Magritte himself, have nevertheless commented on the lasting significance of the two characters of Nick Carter and Nat Pinkerton for the artist. In 1966 Jacques Goossens asked Magritte: 'Have [these characters] influenced your work?' He responded with another kind of denial: 'I don't believe so, because . . . the mystery in these books is a mystery with a key, finally, a mystery that may have a solution. Now, in my work, it's a question of an *unknowable* mystery.'[23]

Fantômas Appears

The notion of an '*unknowable* mystery' provides a key to understanding the importance to Magritte's art of the various biographically significant spaces of illusion and performance – the circus, the fair, the cinema – which we are gradually mapping. One significant enactment of '*unknowable* mystery' is presented by the central character of a very popular film series repeated in cinemas across Brussels during the First World War, the figure of the mysterious arch-criminal Fantômas. These immensely popular silent films, directed by Frenchman Louis Feuillade, were released in 1913–14, and René Navarre, the main actor, became an overnight star. They were based on a series of 32 popular crime novels by Pierre Souvestre and Marcel Allain, published between 1911 and 1913 and translated and distributed across the whole of Europe.

Magritte's interest in Fantômas was shared by many other avant-garde artists and writers, including Juan Gris, André Breton, Yves Tanguy, Guillaume Apollinaire, Max Jacob and Robert Desnos, and the iconic criminal was a recurring element in his work. Adapted for the cinema in 1913, the first showings of the *Fantômas* films at the Cinéma Bleu in Charleroi would certainly have been a significant moment in Magritte's youth. The films were extensively rescreened during the war – *Juve contre Fantômas* in particular was often shown, as indicated by advertisements from April 1918. In addition, Fantômas reappeared in cinemas in 1921 with the release of Edward Sedgwick's American adaptation, which, while less successful than the original series, did keep this criminal character in the popular consciousness. Perhaps the most significant Fantômas image for Magritte's oeuvre features on the cover of the first volume of Souvestre and Allain's novel *Fantômas* in 1911. Magritte painted two versions of this image – one, *The Barbarian* (1927), shows a close-up of a masked, top-hat-wearing Fantômas.

Magritte's turn to this childhood figure occurs at a crucial moment in his life – in September 1927 he and Georgette (joined later by his brother Paul) moved to Paris, following Camille Goemans, who had moved there in April to set up a gallery. Goemans introduced Magritte to the Parisian Surrealists, including Salvador Dalí, Max Ernst, Joan Miró and Hans Arp (for whom Georgette did the stitching on several of his string-relief artworks). Artistically, the stay of almost three years in Paris proved highly productive and innovative – in 1928 alone Magritte completed over a hundred paintings. But in other terms it was a difficult period. They could only afford accommodation in the distant and unfashionable suburb of Le Perreux-sur-Marne, though they stayed occasionally with Goemans in the city centre and Magritte met him and Miró every Thursday for lunch.

Gaining full acceptance into André Breton's Surrealist circle proved a frustrating endeavour. Unlike his fellow Belgians Goemans and Nougé, Magritte was not invited to sign the seminal Surrealist tract 'Permettez!' (Allow Us!) of 23 October 1927.

René Magritte posing with *The Barbarian*, 1938, photograph.

Goemans, who was also Magritte's Paris art dealer, tried to get his paintings into Surrealist galleries and exhibitions, but was rarely successful. And when Breton published his landmark book *Le Surréalisme et la peinture* in 1928, Magritte was conspicuously absent from its pages. In addition, Magritte's 58-year-old father died in 1928 from a stroke, and from early 1929 problems began to amass in the shadow of the growing financial crisis: by the time of the Wall Street crash in October, art had already become difficult to sell, a major reason for the closure in 1930 of the Galerie Goemans, leaving the Magrittes without a monthly income and removing a reliable exhibition space in the capital through which to publicize his work. Galerie Goemans had been advertised in the first (1930) issue of *Cahiers d'art* with the lead artists 'Hans Arp, Salvador Dalí, René Magritte and Yves Tanguy', but the closure followed soon after, and Magritte is notably absent from subsequent issues for several years until a 1935 piece on him by Paul Éluard.[24]

Amid these events, like a bad omen, was a disastrous encounter between Breton and Georgette, precisely at a point where Magritte's Parisian career seemed to be picking up. After their return from their successful holiday with Dalí in Cadaqués, the Magrittes seemed finally to have been embraced by the Parisian Surrealist community. The year closed with the publication of the twelfth and final issue of *La Révolution surréaliste* on 15 December 1929, which included Magritte's propositions about the relations between words and images, 'Les Mots et les images', and a photomontage of photo-booth portraits of the Surrealists. The latter not only included a photo of Magritte, but the photographs were arranged around one of his paintings, *La Femme cachée* (The Hidden Woman), made that year. All the Surrealists' eyes are closed, as if each has uttered the words painted in the painting, 'je ne vois pas la [femme] cachée dans la forêt' (I do not see the [woman] hidden in the forest).

On 14 December 1929, the day before publication, the whole group had gathered at Breton's apartment. Sylvester and Whitfield summarize the scene:

> The essence of the famous story to be drawn from the various accounts – including Georgette Magritte's to ourselves – is that at a gathering of surrealists, Breton noticed that Georgette was wearing a cross on a chain and imperiously demanded the removal of 'that object'. Georgette preferred to leave, and Magritte went with her.[25]

To complicate matters further, it seems that Magritte had recently turned down a job offer in Paris, a decision due largely to Georgette's homesickness for Belgium. In the wake of these events and their economic implications, the couple moved back to Brussels in July 1930, renting the apartment at 135 rue Esseghem, where they lived until 1954. However, the stock market crash also significantly affected the Brussels dealers who had Magritte under contract between 1926 and 1929, leading to the liquidation of their stock. Mesens and Claude Spaak bought up a huge part of Magritte's work for a very low price, temporarily aiding the artist but also creating discord in his subsequent relationship with both men.

Magritte's identification with the master criminal Fantômas, who, camouflaged by his mimicry of bourgeois style, terrorizes Paris as the enemy within, may reflect something of his relationship to the city and its Surrealist circle. In the 1943 painting *The Flame Rekindled* (the title perhaps alluding to his problematic relations with Breton) Magritte depicts Fantômas looming large over the cityscape of Paris, the Eiffel Tower reaching up to his knee, the urban panorama immersed in a threatening, fiery red light. The painting is a near copy of the first Fantômas book's cover image (and John Ashbery argues in his 'Introduction' to the 1986 English translation of Allain and Souvestre's first novel that Fantômas exists 'first of all

René Magritte, *The Flame Rekindled*, c. 1943, oil on canvas.

[as] image'[26]), but Magritte paints a rose in place of the anti-hero's bloodied dagger. The substitution implies a feat of conjuring in which something threatening is both displayed and instantly removed and replaced by something reassuring, thus pulling the audience, who would very likely be familiar with the original cover of the popular novel, in two conflicting directions at once, while the common qualities of each object – in this case the piercing point of

the dagger and the thorns of the rose – sustain a connection between the original and its substitution.

Painted around the start of Magritte's Impressionist period (also known as his Renoir period), which began in 1943, we can detect in *The Flame Rekindled* a covert expression of solidarity by the Belgian artist with a symbol of French culture – a significant gesture in the period when both France and Belgium were under German occupation during the Second World War. Again, we can trace the origins of this painting back to Magritte's teenage years, potentially to a very specific moment. The 16 March 1911 issue of the Belgian newspaper *Le Peuple* carried an advertisement on page six promoting the volume *Juve contre Fantômas*. Situated on the bottom left side of the page amid small printed ads for asthma and constipation medication and beside a picture of a gramophone, the three-dimensional illusion of this advertisement gives it the appearance of something solid pasted onto the page, immediately capturing the reader's attention. The image is, of course, the one of Fantômas towering over the city of Paris, dagger in one hand and chin resting pensively in the other. His gaze confronts the viewer while the large letters placed above and below him shout out his name in different typescripts. These elements animate the image, and the page would certainly have captured a thirteen-year-old Magritte's attention and imagination. The bold, capitalized letters of FANTÔMAS also featured distinctly elsewhere, in cinema advertisements carried by Belgian newspapers like *La Meuse* in 1913 and 1914, while the cinematic version of *Juve contre Fantômas* was shown in October 1913 across Belgium, with screenings in Brussels, Saint-Gilles, Vilvorde and Molenbeek in '4 partiés, 46 tableaux' (4 parts and 46 scenes) format with matinees at 1.30 p.m. and evening screenings at 8.30 p.m.[27]

The style and *mises en scène* of the *Fantômas* films impacted on the prominence in Magritte's work of recognizably cinematic screens and framing devices, a feature originating around 1925 or

1926 as he develops a conception of the frame as a space containing not an opening on to some other space (the grounding illusion of representational pictorialism, in which the pictorial frame works as if it were a window opening out on to the scene depicted), but instead a surface onto which is projected, from somewhere behind the viewer and outside the frame, an image. This conception involves a transformation of the Surrealist notion of 'mystery', which was also a central conceptual element of the *Fantômas* narratives. Surrealist art makes extensive use of frames to connote this mystery through the implication of another reality beyond or behind that of the image. However, there is nothing 'beyond' the staged illusions that Magritte's paintings construct. Like those of the master criminal whose crimes are unsolvable, presenting their victims and the investigating police with baffling enigmas, the conundrums they present reside precisely in their refusal of the possibility of a space outside that constructed in the painting.

The first and most obvious incorporation of a recognizably cinematic scene into Magritte's paintings – and one which draws on Feuillade's characteristic directorial style of constructing scenes through the effect of layered depth – is *The Murderer Threatened* (1927), which, perhaps not coincidentally, was at that time the largest painting he had produced.[28] As Sylvester and Whitfield observe, the painting draws directly on a scene in Feuillade's third *Fantômas* film, *Le Mort qui tue* (The Murderous Corpse, 1913), in which two criminals stand at either side of a doorway waiting to catch their victim with a net.[29] In Magritte's painting they become two bowler-hatted men preparing to burst in upon a bizarre scene in which we appear to be witnessing the aftermath of a domestic murder – in a wooden-floored room a nude female figure lies prone atop some kind of chaise longue, while a suited male figure adjusts the controls on a gramophone, a suitcase on the floor beside him and some clothing draped over a chair in the foreground. At the rear of this scene, what appears to be a window frames a

René Magritte, *The Murderer Threatened*, 1927, oil on canvas.

mountainous landscape while three male heads peer in, viewing from the reverse perspective the scene we witness. For all its aura of menace and impending violence (one of the bowler-hatted men brandishes a club) the painting is curiously static, evoking not so much a film still as a cryptic scene of accidental and embarrassing intrusion on some kind of Kafkaesque private absurdity.

The Murderer Threatened combines its cinematic reference points with a series of allusions to pictorial art, on which critics tend to concentrate. The image's spatial structure seems to derive from the perspectival architectural arrangements characteristic of De Chirico.[30] However, the background element of the three men peering through the window adapts Max Ernst's painting *The Virgin Spanking the Christ Child before Three Witnesses: A. B., P. É., and the Painter* (1926), itself a play on Piero della Francesca's three witnesses in *The Baptism of Christ* (*c.* 1444–50).[31] Ernst's abbreviations, referring to André Breton and Paul Éluard, suggest that Magritte has incorporated into his painting a further element of critical reference, positioning the three Surrealists of Ernst's painting squarely within his own work as material witnesses to an apparent crime, their perspective mirroring ours rather than being afforded a privileged or transcendent insight into the pictorial scene. Or perhaps they are merely part of the image Magritte depicts as projected onto the rear wall, mere elements accidentally present in a landscape lacking in depth, part of the rearmost plane of the image's layering of scenic components.

The painting is effectively a collage of allusions to material deriving from a variety of cultural levels from popular to avant-garde, exemplifying Max Ernst's observation about Magritte's pictures being 'collages entirely painted by hand'.[32] This referential layering seems to be mirrored by a spatial one, which draws on the use in Feuillade's films of 'layered depth',[33] the arrangement of elements in the film image to suggest perspective and sequentiality. Magritte's spatial layering introduces (cinematic) sequentiality into the scene, constructing a strange dimensionality (redolent of Picasso's *papiers collés*) in which is presented a single, momentary scene in a space connoting a time sequence surrounding that recorded moment. In Feuillade's film, the two criminals flank a double door: one side is shut and through the open half two people enter. The space where the next scene happens is constructed as being in front of us. Magritte's painting omits this open space, that of the enclosed scene. Instead we are positioned as onlookers to a scene framed by what appears to be the proscenium of a stage, with the two criminals literally waiting in the wings. The flatness of the apparent window with the onlookers at the back of the dramatic stage transforms it into the backdrop of a stage. If we are looking onto the scene and a performance within it, we are also looked at by the three characters who are clearly part of this backdrop, raising questions about who is performing, what is performed and for whom.

Cinema Non-stop

Magritte makes clear his penchant for cinema in many comments from the 1940s onwards. He expresses a particular liking for films that make no claim to the moral high ground:

> the 'moral' cinema is not cinema: it is a boring caricature about a boring lecture on morals. Like the moral lecture, it's lacking morals. As true cinema, I regard films such as: *Coup dur chez les mous* [Hard Strike on a Soft Target; dir. Jean Loubignac, 1956], *Madame et son auto* [Madame and her Car; dir. Robert Vernay, 1958], *Babette s'en va-t-en guerre* [Babette Goes to War; dir. Christian-Jacque, 1959]. 'True' because no demand other than to amuse us, has robbed these films of morality.[34]

Magritte's comments, helpfully recorded by André Blavier, reveal a number of films he saw, including Fritz Lang's film noir *The Woman in the Window* (1944), Lewis Allen's *The Uninvited* (1944), Louis Daquin's *Le Point du jour* (The Mark of the Day; 1949), Pierre Etaix's *Le Soupirant* (The Suitor; 1962); and some he was less impressed by, such as Vsevolod Pudovkin's *Admiral Nakhimov* (1947), John Emerson's *The Americano* (1916), François Truffaut's *Les Quatre Cents Coups* (The 400 Blows; 1959), Jacques Deray's *Symphonie pour un massacre* (1963) and Georges Lautner's 1962 *L'Oeil du monocle* (which Magritte thought was 'unbearable').[35] Magritte was a big John Wayne fan, apparently less interested in Marilyn Monroe, expressed a dislike for and disinterest in James Bond and had some enthusiasm for Hitchcock (whom he misspelled Hichkoc) – mentioning films such as *The Paradine Case* (1947) and *Psycho* (1960) and calling the director 'an imbecile with great talent'.[36] Such generic preferences indicate a taste for the darker side of film history, but not the visceral excess of horror cinema.

A key painting in the development of Magritte's particular brand of Surrealist screen imagery was painted in the same month as *Cinéma bleu*. *Nocturne* seems to be the work in which Magritte engages most fully with the cinematic image and its potential to perform one of his favourite visual tricks, namely the dissolution of the relation between outside and inside. Here, the dramatic scene is surrounded by curtain folds, giving the clearest suggestion yet that the interiors Magritte was composing during this period are versions of the space of the movie theatre. The painting combines elements clearly influenced by the camera obscura (discussed in the next chapter) and Plato's allegory of the cave, relocating them to a more clearly cinematic space – a dark red curtain frames the right-hand side of an interior with a mottled dark blue and white backdrop (a wall or another curtain?) to the rear and a pale brown patterned floor (reminiscent both of the geodesic forms depicted on the floor of *The Lost Jockey* and of a browned leaf flattened out, as if the interior space were at once constructed and natural). Within this space, a white *bilboquet* stands like a sentinel before a rectangular screen on which we see a dark, stormy landscape with, at its centre, a burning house. The *bilboquet* is stringed and decorated with S-holes as if it were a distorted violin (a motif possibly borrowed from Picasso's collages; a similar counterpoint of image and motif, in which a human head transforms into a musical instrument, can be seen in Magritte's 1928 *Portrait of P.-G. Van Hecke*). The border between the framed image and the interior – the edge of the frame – is crossed at its upper left-hand corner by a flying dove, seemingly composed of the same red material as the curtain. The entire painting presents an allegory of cinematic performance bringing together the darkened space, the screen image, the dynamic tension between monumental stasis of the viewing object and the space that contains it, and the implicit motion of flames and dove associated with the screen. These elements all combine

within the careful overlapping of planes and layers, arranged
in sequential movements, as the viewing eye tracks across the
painting to produce the mobile effect: curtain-space-frame-image;
dove-*bilboquet*-floor-backdrop.

Nocturne is in many ways a transitional image, incorporating
elements characteristic of that phase of Magritte's career but
gesturing forward (via the dove and the flames) to what will become
key motifs of his later works. In a later painting, *The Perfect Image*
(1928), a woman is shown looking at what appears to be a frame
surrounded by darkness, a scene evoking the darkened screen in
an auditorium before the film begins. *The Perfect Image* reworks
Nocturne, replacing the *bilboquet* with a female head, introducing
clearly into the image's rhetoric the analysis of spectatorship that
seems to concern much of Magritte's painting. Both images are

René Magritte, *Nocturne*, 1925, oil on canvas.

René Magritte, *Bather between Light and Darkness*, 1936, oil on canvas.

concerned with looking and with how the frame functions as
both screen and container of the viewed image. Similarly, in the
1936 painting *Bather between Light and Darkness* (which reworks
an older, more Cubist picture, *Bather* of 1925, contemporaneous
with *Nocturne* and *Cinéma bleu*) Magritte depicts a female nude in
an austere interior. Eyes closed, head resting on her right arm, she
is lying on a white surface before a dark wall on which is painted
a framed seascape, its layered waves both static and expressive
of latent movement. In front of the nude Magritte has placed an
enigmatic black sphere, an object of her silent meditation.

Magritte may be drawing here on the experience of viewing
Harold L. Muller's silent film *There It Is*, also made in 1928. This
comedy, a remarkable compendium of cinematic special effects,
visual puns, jokes and illusions, shows a Scotland Yard detective,
Charley MacNeesha (played by Charles R. Bowers), and his stop-
motion-animated bug assistant MacGregor in New York City trying
to solve the mystery of the 'Fuzz-Faced Phantom' who is wreaking

havoc in a household. Pots float across rooms and a pair of trousers dance around of their own accord atop a dresser. Magritte's painting echoes the sequence in which a framed seascape becomes animated, the waves moving around in the picture frame until they splash out of the painting and onto a sleeping MacGregor, who immediately opens an umbrella.

Magritte incorporated cinematic references and scenes into his paintings throughout his career. One of the best-known of these references is *Homage to Mack Sennett* (1936, the same year as *Bather between Light and Darkness*), which namechecks the famous American slapstick comedy film-maker Mack Sennett (1880–1960). Known as the 'King of Comedy', Sennett co-founded the Keystone production company in 1912 and would discover and promote comedians such as Ben Turpin, Fatty Arbuckle, Carole Lombard, W. C. Fields, Bing Crosby and, perhaps most importantly, Charlie Chaplin. *Homage to Mack Sennett* (which Magritte reworks in 1948 in the painting *Philosophie dans le boudoir*, adopting a title from the Marquis de Sade) is nearly entirely filled by the image of a wardrobe or cupboard, its left door open to reveal an empty nightgown embellished with some of the features of the body that inhabited it, suggesting a blurring of the boundaries between inside and outside or container and contained.

During an interview with Jean Neyens in 1965, Magritte described what he claimed was his first memory: 'The first feeling I can remember was, that I lay in my cradle, and the first thing I saw was a cupboard beside my cradle, the world showed itself to me in the form of a cupboard.'[37] *Homage to Mack Sennett* clearly plays with the slippages of meaning and perception implied by this memory. The image's uncanny effects lie in its assertion of a symbolic union between cupboard and coffin as places for storing clothes and bodies, its allusion to the expression 'skeletons in the cupboard', and the condensation of nightgown and female body. The key motif, however – and a gesture towards the dynamism of revelation in the painting – is the right wardrobe door, which resembles an empty picture frame, echoing the frame that contains (or is contained by) the picture itself; that on the left, half open, reveals what is inside the wardrobe. The various frames that organize the pictorial space suggest a philosophical statement about how picture frames, wardrobes and coffins all serve in different ways as means of incarceration.[38]

The painting and its titular reference to Mack Sennett can be connected to a comic scene from *Won in a Cupboard*, a silent film directed by the American Mabel Normand and produced by Sennett in 1914 (and probably screened in Belgium at the time). The film was only recently rediscovered, with several other lost films, in New Zealand. Its plot concerns a burgeoning romance, in which Mabel (Normand herself) meets, 'as if by magic' (as a scene caption announces), Charles Avery. Her father (Charles Inslee) discovers Avery's mother (Alice Davenport) inappropriately hidden in a cupboard. Mabel and Charles arrive, and the parents discover that the two are lovers, before finding themselves in the awkward situation of hiding in a cupboard, trying to keep the doors shut. Mabel and Charles think that a tramp has hidden in the cupboard, and they run for assistance, generating further chaos. Amid much clowning and slapstick, help arrives and the cupboard is heaved into the garden, in a typically Magrittean inside–outside reversal.

In the next scene the camera focuses on the cupboard, which suddenly fills the screen. This image clearly resembles Magritte's own painterly 'close-up' of the cupboard. After the people outside try to break the cupboard door down, a solution is found – one of the men puts a hose into a broken panel in the door, spraying the two inside and forcing them out of the cupboard. They emerge, their heads covered in soaked white clothes that had been hanging in the cupboard. A shot showing one of the two coming out of the half-open cupboard is the point alluded to by Magritte's painting, which transforms the wet figure, head covered by a clinging white cloth,

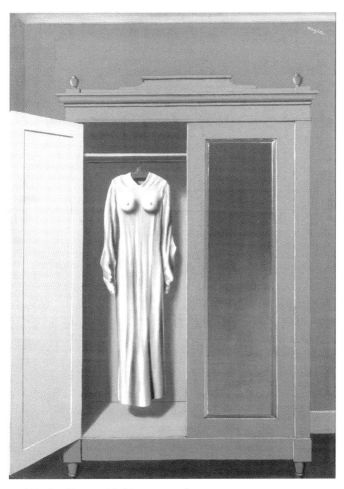

René Magritte, *Homage to Mack Sennett*, 1936, oil on canvas.

A scene from *Won in a Cupboard* (1914), directed by Mabel Normand.

into a nightgown. This scene of the two figures' cloth-covered heads is also a major source for Magritte's famous 1927 painting *The Lovers*, which shows two people (their clothing suggests they are a man and a woman) kissing, their heads veiled by white cloth, its folds tightly wrapped, resembling wet towels.

These references to imagery found in popular cinema indicate how Magritte's conceptions of the uncanny or unsettling – enacted in a series of key rhetorical tropes including radical displacements and inversions or reversals, incongruous juxtapositions, monumental disparities of size and scale, and sudden disruptive emergences of inappropriate or unexpected objects in familiar spaces – may derive in large part from the development and display of special cinematic effects he saw in movies. They also reveal another important aspect of Magritte's work: having painted *The Lovers* in 1928 and *Homage to Mack Sennett* in 1936, we can deduce that Magritte returned to the resources of imagery provided by films like *Won in a Cupboard* (which he probably saw as a teenager, suggesting a long shelf life for its imagery), reusing different elements of it for a variety of purposes throughout his career. This suggests a particular kind of film memory at work in Magritte's conception of the potential utility of cinema as an image resource.

Another example of Magritte's use of cinematic imagery – referencing a technique that he probably witnessed at a much younger age and 'stored' as a resource for future use – can be seen in the painting *The Impatient Ones* (1928). Once again darkness dominates the image, surrounding two erratically framed male figures, possibly wrestlers or boxers, and the stage they perform on.[39] However, another source for this painting could be cinematic, as sports and acrobatic events were frequently screened in cinemas. The painting's dance-like representation of wrestlers set against a dark void with only a moon-like light shining above them seems to derive from a short film made in 1895 by the German brothers Max and Emil Skladanowsky entitled *Greiner versus Sandow: Ringkämpfer* (Wrestlers), which for the first time captured a wrestling bout

René Magritte, *The Lovers*, 1928, oil on canvas.

René Magritte, *The Impatient Ones*, 1928, oil on canvas.

on celluloid. Drawing on Eadweard Muybridge's stop-motion photographs of sportsmen, the film frames the wrestlers as engaged in a graceful dance, the moves and geometries enhanced and sharpened by the emptiness of the dark void surrounding them. The moon of Magritte's painting would thus be revealed to be a spotlight. The Skladanowskys invented the Bioscop, a projection technology which was used to display the first moving picture show to a paying audience on 1 November 1895, just before the debut of the Lumière Brothers' Cinématographe. Their films toured widely in Europe and Scandinavia, and as a young boy Magritte may well have seen them.

Surrealism in/on Film

Cinema clearly influenced Magritte in important ways, and the works he produced around 1928 bear traces of the connections between his cinematic experiences and his involvement in the Parisian Surrealist movement at that time. The influence also worked the other way, as Magritte's images partly inspiring the two great Surrealist films of Salvador Dalí and Luis Buñuel, *Un Chien andalou* (1929) and *L'Âge d'or* (1930). Camille Goemans introduced Dalí, Buñuel, Magritte and other Belgian artists and intellectuals to each other in 1929.[40] Joan Minguet Batllori demonstrates the closeness of these relations at the time by identifying a postcard from 28 April 1929, sent by Dalí to his friend the Catalan art critic Sebastià Gasch, which shows a view of the Carnot square in the village of Bry-sur-Marne; it was stamped in Le Perreux-sur-Marne, suggesting that Dalí visited the Magrittes there, and may even have stayed with them occasionally. The postcard also indicates a wider network of social relations, as Dalí invites the friends with whom he shared his Parisian stay – Buñuel, René and Georgette, Goemans and his partner Yvonne Bernard, and Armand Bernard (who was to become orchestra conductor for *L'Âge d'or*) – to follow him in signing the postcard. 'Those signatures placed randomly on the postcard', writes Minguet Batllori,

> allow us to corroborate the intense contact that Buñuel and Dalí maintained with the group which was to become called the Belgian Surrealists during the period of realization of *Un chien andalou*. It would also explain to some extent the surprising presence of iconographic motifs in the film that come from Magritte's paintings of 1927 and 1928.[41]

In August 1929 Dalí invited the Magrittes to holiday in Cadaqués, a fishing village on the Catalonian coast where his family had a house. Georgette later told Sylvester that four of them travelled there together: René and Georgette, Goemans and his companion Yvonne Bernard, accompanied by the Magrittes' German spitz dogs, Loulou and Doumi (the couple owned a succession of these dogs, most named Loulou). They were joined by Buñuel, the poet and co-founder of French Surrealism Paul Éluard and his wife Gala.[42]

Dalí and Buñuel's *Un Chien andalou* draws strongly on imagery Magritte was developing around 1928. The scene in which Simone Mareuil sits staring rapt into a book evokes Magritte's *The Subjugated Reader* of 1928, and the image of Pierre Batcheff's character staring at his hand derives almost wholly from *The Mysterious Suspicion* of the same year. The French poster for the film shows scenes and titles arranged in six framed compartments, recalling Magritte's cinematic frame-by-frame images and framing strategies such as he used in *Man with a Newspaper* (1928). The painting's four frames each reproduce the same interior, with the exception of the first, which additionally includes a man seated at a table (a scene Magritte has derived from an illustration in Dr F. E. Bilz's *Das neue Naturheilverfahren* (The New Naturopathy) of 1895, the year cinema was born).

In 1928 Magritte produced several examples of this serial form of depicting individually framed image-elements, with the frames sometimes presented separately against a background, sometimes connected together into irregularly shaped bundles of framed spaces. Sometimes he painted words in the frames instead of images, such as in *The Empty Mask*, where the words *ciel* (sky), *corps humain (ou forêt)* (human body (in the forest)), *rideau* (curtains) and *façade de maison* (house facade) offer a reverse rebus, a kind of verbal mapping of an imagined picture within its visual field. The painting is a game of verbal–visual suggestion, as well as an exploration of the distinctions between pictorial and written representation. Magritte's use of words also recalls the caption frames used in silent

René Magritte, *The Mysterious Suspicion*, 1928, oil on canvas.

films to represent speech or develop narrative events. In the film
Les Rivaux d'Arnheim (The Rivals of Arnheim; dir. Henri Adreani,
1912), brief captions containing only an article and a noun, such as
'La Discord', fill the black screen, in a style that Magritte's paintings
clearly resemble.

L'Âge d'or, the second and final film collaboration between
Dalí and Buñuel, also drew extensively on their many exchanges
with Magritte and other Surrealists. Its narrative form derives
from the cut-up works of Benjamin Peret, and several Surrealists
(including Max Ernst) make cameo appearances. In keeping with
Dalí's paradoxical conviction (expressed in 1932) that 'the more
"cinematic" cinema is, the more it is to be deplored,'[43] the film's
iconography overtly alludes to a number of painterly Magrittean
themes. In one scene, a bowler-hatted man with a stick, seen from
behind in a typically Magrittean composition, effortlessly carries
what looks like a rock on his head, an image counterpointed by
a statue wearing a rock on its head. A windy, moving skyscape
appears in the frames of a mirror and magically escapes these
frames, the wind blowing out into the face of the main female
character (played by Lya Lys), who gazes into the mirror in the style
of a Magritte figure. *L'Âge d'or* owes much to Buñuel's obsession
with Hollywood imagery, but it is also indebted to Magritte's
repertoire of static, often uncanny images, which enable the success
of many of the film's conceits.

Cinema offered a crucial resource from which Magritte borrowed
significant elements of the image repertoire he would use throughout
his life, extending it in response to new conceptions of the intellectual
significance of the screen. In *Shéhérazade* (1947) he introduces a new
motif, a disembodied pair of female eyes and lips (adorned with
bright red lipstick), framed decoratively by an arrangement of pearls,
standing (in this first version) on a low plinth with a glass of water on
its left, while the background consists of a mixture of white clouds
and ethereal but solid arches receding upwards. A theatrical curtain

René Magritte, *Shéhérazade*, 1947, oil on canvas.

is visible to the right, as are two tall, pointed pyramid forms. The painting contains multiple elements deriving from or reminiscent of other works by Magritte.

The pearled face returns in a series of subsequent works, such as a 1948 version of *Shéhérazade* where the face and the glass are placed in a landscape mixed with gigantic curtains and conspicuously taking on an increasingly stage-like appearance. In 1950 the face reappears before a seascape, and in the 1953 mural in the Grande Casino Knokke, *The Enchanted Domain*, the pearly face is held by 'the tramp' – another recurring figure, a self-portrait of Magritte (and probably a nod to Chaplin) in which the upper body has been replaced by a dove-filled cage. This pearly face alludes to the full lips and wide, grey eyes surrounded by pearls of Yvonne De Carlo in Walter Reisch's American musical *Song of Scheherazade* (1947), based on the life of the Russian composer Nikolai Rimsky-Korsakov (played by Jean-Pierre Aumont) and his brief affair in 1865 with a Spanish cabaret dancer named Cara de Talavera, played by De Carlo.

Magritte's pearl-outlined facial image reworks the pearl headdress De Carlo wears in the film, an adornment mirrored in the pearl-like shine of her eyes and on her lips, a feature visible in one of the stills which may have hung in cinema corridors and display cases to promote the film. We might also note that the opposing C-shapes depicted at the base of Magritte's pearl arrangements resemble the pearl-encrusted logo of the fashion house Chanel, suggesting that Magritte has covertly incorporated commercial imagery into his paintings. *Song of Scheherazade* was made by Universal Studios, whose own distinctive logo (featuring a rotating planet Earth hanging in space) seems also to have entered Magritte's image repertoire – in the series of images titled *The Great Style* he produced from 1951 onwards, Magritte paints a similar floating globe, sometimes attached to or resting atop a plant, contrasting mass with airy weightlessness. A different version produced in the same year, *Striking a Different Note*, pairs the globe with a huge apple (or a tiny

Yvonne De Carlo in Walter Reisch's *Song of Scheherazade* (1947).

Earth with a normal-sized apple), playing again with perspective and juxtaposition and introducing by connotation (with Isaac Newton and the apple) the theme of gravity.

Black Magic (1934) also becomes significant when viewed through a cinematic lens. In this painting a nude is shown whose top half is painted a graduated blue, creating the visual effect of her body seeming to transform or dissolve into the sky behind her. This and similar dissolutions in Magritte's paintings clearly draw on cinematic effects like the fade or the wipe, in which a scene dissolves or is 'wiped' across the screen to reveal another. Some of the most expressive examples of this can be found in Jean Epstein's 1923 French drama *Coeur fidèle* (Faithful Heart), in which fades are used to introduce notions of yearning and distance, memory and loss. In a scene which seems to have influenced Magritte's painting, the face of the female protagonist, Marie (Gina Manès), dissolves into a seascape. While conventional spatial logic might

René Magritte, *Black Magic*, 1934, oil on canvas.

Scene from *Coeur fidèle* (Faithful Heart; 1923), directed by Jean Epstein.

indicate that, in the fade, the second image is somehow *behind* the first and thus revealed when the first image is erased or fades away, the qualities of the cinematic movement-image clearly locate the second scene temporally *after* the first.[44] The fade/wipe is thus a kind of visual trick facilitated by the film's introduction of time and movement into the image – precisely the kind of cinematic magic that charmed Magritte.

4

From Camera Obscura to Panoramic Vision

Returning from Paris in 1930, Magritte suffered a creative block and was for a while unable to paint, but he was warmly welcomed back into the artistic scene in Brussels and, with Georgette and Paul, established Studio Dongo. Nevertheless he pined for the lost friendship with Breton and Éluard, who also regretted the split. In 1932 they sent Magritte copies of their latest books inscribed 'To René Magritte/ in memory of the time when he was my friend/ Paul Éluard' and 'To René Magritte/ his friend in spite of himself/ André Breton'. The reconciliation, albeit temporary, came in early 1933 when Breton wrote to Nougé, Mesens and Magritte asking them to contribute to the final number of the Parisian Surrealist publication *Le Surréalisme au service de la révolution*. Magritte contributed the two-canvas painting *On the Threshold of Liberty*, and his inclusion in the major Surrealist exhibition in June 1933 at the Parisian Galerie Pierre Colle signalled the end of the feud. When Breton moved to America in 1941 he included a paragraph on Magritte in an essay published in the second edition of *Le Surréalisme et la peinture*, and Marcel Duchamp convinced him to use Magritte's second version of *The Red Model* (1935) on the book's cover.

From the early 1930s onwards Magritte worked in Brussels, developing his preoccupation with optical tricks and illusions in a series of images that have become iconically 'Magrittean' in their depiction of canvases seemingly replacing or hiding something 'behind' them, elaborating the question of the painting's 'beyond' touched upon in the previous chapter. The illusionism involved in these images marks the beginning of Magritte's critique of painterly representation as a kind of trickery, a critique closely connected to his involvement during the 1930s and early 1940s in left-wing politics (discussed in the next chapter). While the caricature of Magritte as the discreetly charming, eccentric, bowler-hatted bourgeois man was clearly fostered by his own multiple self-representations in writing, painting and photography, that image masks a rather more subversive element in his character, which finds expression in works that relentlessly challenge conventional viewpoints and perspectives, demanding a wholesale rethink of what actually constitutes our conception of art.

Camera Obscura

Magritte's illusionism draws in part on his understanding of the effects achieved through cinematic projection, but he also exploits the visual effects achieved by another, older kind of visual projection, that of the camera obscura, which enabled the projection of external views onto the internal walls of a darkened room. *The Fair Captive* (1931) is the earliest of these paintings, depicting a landscape containing a canvas on which is reproduced the fragment of the landscape that the canvas obscures. Critics have noted the striking relationship between this painting and a set of diagrams from the textbook *Traité pratique de perspective* by Armand Cassagne – a book in use at the Académie Royale des Beaux-Arts in Brussels in the five years that Magritte was studying there from October 1916.[1] However, once we shift perspective to consider the influence of the camera obscura on Magritte's conventional trope of exterior spaces internalized, a different

René Magritte, *The Fair Captive*, 1931, oil on canvas.

relation between image as ground and image as figure emerges.
Rather than seeing differences between a landscape and the space
of the canvas seemingly reproducing the slice of landscape it
hides (external landscape, internal canvas), we can start to see the
landscape as, in fact, a projection onto an interior wall in front of
which is a white canvas – the latter thus becoming a protruding
element of the surface the image is projected on. The projected
image doesn't differentiate between wall and canvas except for the
places it doesn't reach, such as the slim, white, nail-dotted line at
the left of the canvas frame, the clip holding the canvas in place and
the slight outline of the canvas edges – that is, those elements used
by Magritte to produce the three-dimensional perspectival effect
that matches the literal element of the picture (a canvas standing
in the landscape represented on the canvas). This outline of the
canvas edge would not occur in a natural environment, but would
be seen in a projection that outlines certain parts of objects not
bearing the projected image, allowing us to read these images as
mimicking camera-obscura projections onto walls in front of which

stand bare picture frames on easels. The canvas edge functions like a hinge, emphasizing the deception of a canvas exactly reproducing that which is behind it, while also revealing the canvas as distinct from its environment, a representation superimposed on the real. Like a magic trick, it deceives while simultaneously asserting that we are witnessing a deception. While (like all these paintings) *The Fair Captive* teases the viewer by inviting them to look behind the canvas *before* them, reading the image as the product of a camera-obscura projection reveals that it is precisely *behind* them, at the hidden source of the projection, that Magritte's act of creative deception takes place. A radical shift of viewer perspective enables us to reverse conventional figure–ground relations so that ground becomes figure and vice versa, altering the way in which Magritte's painting works to disconcert the viewer and create its unsettling effects.

Magritte reworked this optical effect in *The Human Condition*, a painting from 1933 whose theme and title he adapted and repeated in a number of paintings throughout his career. The title, possibly alluding to Rousseau's 'Our [that is, philosophers and artists] true study is that of the human condition,'[2] also echoes that of a novel published the same year by the French novelist and art critic André Malraux. The painting is a development of *The Fair Captive* (indeed, transmitted light and infrared photographs taken by the National Gallery of Art in Washington, DC, have revealed that Magritte originally incorporated a part of *The Fair Captive*, a thin line of houses, into this image, which he then painted over) in which the easel and the spectator are positioned inside a room, looking out on to a landscape. It shows an easel standing in front of a window, seemingly reproducing the very thing that would appear behind it in the view outside the room. Magritte famously commented on the problem of how a painting may conceal something within it: 'Behind the colours in the pictures is the canvas. Behind the canvas there is a wall, behind the wall there is . . . etc. Visible things always hide other visible things. But a visible image hides nothing.'³ (This comment reads like the statements of a magician during the set-up or 'pledge' of a magic trick, a connotation to which we will later return.)

A thin dotted line at the edge of the canvas, together with the easel legs and a slight overlap of the canvas with the interior curtain, is a key marker of the illusory character of this scene, and is conventionally read as a marker for a canvas standing in front of the window. Yet, as in *The Fair Captive*, it is this dotted line that creates the illusion that leads us to think about how canvas (apparent figure) and landscape (apparent ground) relate to each other; the painterly illusion that there is an outside, and an inside that replaces or stands in for it. As with the previous painting, once we shift our perspective to the landscape being an image projected from behind the position of the viewer, we grasp that there is no 'outside' but simply projection from inside. The conundrum of what replaces or stands in for what – the puzzle that critics conventionally ascribe to these paintings – resolves into a flat surface or screen upon which the image is projected.

Magritte's elaboration on this painting in his 'Lifeline 1' lecture in 1938 reinforces the conventional reading of these images as deceptions by concealment. By focusing attention on what he calls 'the problem of the window' he leads the viewer to pay attention to that which is in front of a window while also being behind a canvas (which seemingly blocks and reproduces at the same time the view):

> The problem of the window gave rise to *The Human Condition*. In front of a window seen from the inside of a room, I placed a picture representing exactly the section of the landscape hidden by the picture. The tree represented in the picture therefore concealed the tree behind it, outside the room. For the spectator, it was both inside the room in the picture and, at the same time, conceptually outside in the real landscape. This is how we see the world, we see it outside ourselves and

yet the only representation we have of it is inside us. Similarly, we sometimes place in the past something which is happening in the present. In this case, time and space lose that crude meaning which is the only one they have in everyday life.[4]

According to this logic, representation is a kind of concealment: that which is inside both represents and conceals that which is outside, and perception (of what is outside the room, seen by a viewing subject) merges with conception (the construction within the viewing subject of an interpretation of the exterior world) to produce, within the painting, 'how we see the world'. The implications of this argument were not lost on Magritte. He is alert to how the complex processes of perception and conception interact to produce our cognition of reality, and understands that external realities are products of internal processes of perception and conception ('we see it outside ourselves and yet the only representation we have of it is inside us'). The 'outside' objects of the real, objective world are thus, in Magritte's reading of these images, displaced (and, in this displacement, transformed) into 'the inside' products of human cognition.

Magritte's comment seems to work like a central element of the practice of stage magic, the use of misdirection. The magician uses a range of cues to direct attention away from where the actual trick is happening. It leads us to pay attention to the thing before us – for example, the canvas hiding a 'real' landscape – while the actual process that creates the picture is happening somewhere else (behind us, or – in reverse-projection – behind the wall we are looking at), an impression achieved through a painterly version of the image-effect of a camera obscura. Similarly, in *Blood-letting* (1938–9), a picture frame hanging on an interior wall (perhaps a gallery wall) contains an image of a brick wall. While the viewer, following Magritte's comments in 'Lifeline 1', concocts a narrative about this painting's concerns with representation and reality, and how these map on to

Magritte's cryptic explanations ('Behind the canvas there is a wall, behind the wall there is . . . etc.'), we could instead interpret the brick wall as in fact a projection onto a flat surface, leading us to the conclusion that there was indeed never anything behind the painted wall, but only an image projected onto it.

The conjuror's 'misdirection' practised by Magritte in leading the viewer's attention to what is in front of them – preoccupying them with relations of outside–inside and painted canvas and landscape – positions the viewers themselves within a scenario reminiscent of that imagined by Plato in his famous allegory of the cave. Plato imagined the human condition (hence, perhaps, the title Magritte chose for his 1933 painting) as akin to people living in an underground cave, shackled so that they cannot turn their heads but can only stare at a wall before them, unaware of the opening of the cave behind them. In this restricted position they come to believe that they are staring at something real, while all they observe are shadows projected onto the wall from outside the cave, cast by objects – themselves copies of ideas – passed before a fire.[5]

Magritte was aware of Plato's allegory as he maintained a significant interest in philosophy throughout his life. His library at the time of his death was catalogued by Sylvester and included several volumes of translation and commentary on Plato, including André Cresson's *Plato* and his introduction to *Ancient Philosophy* from *Que sais-je?* (a popular series of short introductions for lay readers); volumes II, III and V of the *Complete Works* of Plato (in Émile Chambry's translation); and Walter Pater's *Plato and Platonism*. He owned many other books from the *Que sais-je?* series – including Paul Foulquié's introduction to dialectics and Jean-François Lyotard's volume on phenomenology – as well as a *Selected Works* of Descartes, Henry Duméry's *Phenomenology and Religion*, several volumes by Hegel (including the *Phenomenology of Spirit*, *Lectures on the History of Philosophy* and *Proofs of the Existence of God*), two copies of Immanuel Kant's

Critique of Pure Reason (a marginal comment by Sylvester suggests one was 'prob. much read'), volumes by Louis Lavelle including his *Introduction to Ontology*, and Pascal's *Pensées*. He also owned numerous books on Martin Heidegger and existentialism, including copies of *The Essence of Truth*, a collection of Heidegger's 1932 lectures on Plato.[6]

Magritte's engagement with Plato's allegory of the cave is explicit in the 1935 version of *The Human Condition*, where the painting's elements of cave, opening and fire, and its thematic concern with representation (an easel representing the thing it hides) closely resemble the philosopher's content and themes. Magritte notes in a letter to Paul Éluard from December 1935:

> I am also re-doing a variant of *The Human Condition* but seen this time in a cave such as smugglers might use; in a corner of the cave there will be a fire and the landscape will be mountainous; the picture standing on the easel will show the continuation of the landscape and an old castle on the edge of a precipice.[7]

René Magritte, *The Human Condition*, 1935, oil on canvas.

While Magritte's theoretical statements imply a looking-forward towards the landscape in front of us in order to conceptualize this painting, it may be that turning backwards reveals another level. The opening and its clear outline once again appear like a camera-obscura projection on a wall with a canvas in front of it, suggesting that we are, just like Plato's shackled people, still seeing a projected image rather than 'reality'.

The significance of these concerns is developed in later paintings. *Personal Values* (1952) depicts a skyscape appearing on the walls of a room, again resembling the camera-obscura effect of projecting the external view into an internal space. This painting develops the conceit of works like 1928's *The Secret Life*, in which a room contains another skyscape, its artifice or projected character emphasized by its clear delineation along the cornices. Magritte offered *Personal Values* to Alexander Iolas, a highly regarded ballet soloist who retired in the mid-1940s to open the Hugo Gallery in New York. Not long after the opening, Iolas and Magritte established contact to discuss sales and exhibitions, and soon Iolas became Magritte's art dealer. Edward James's strong promotion of Magritte's work might have helped in bringing him to the attention of Iolas and other dealers and gallerists. Magritte's second American one-man show, featuring 22 works (the first fifteen of which were replicas, having been held in 1936 at New York's Julien Levy Gallery), opened at the Hugo Gallery in 1947, after a delay due to the apparent unsaleability of the works he produced in what is known as his 'Impressionist' period (a continuation of his interest in Renoir, expressed earlier in *La Loge*), which Magritte practised from 1943 to 1947.

The economic pressure of the art market (and strong encouragement from Iolas, whose interests lay in increasing Magritte's marketability) turned Magritte away from this style to resume his better-known one. This pressure is also clear in Iolas's remark to Magritte about *Personal Values* in a letter of 15 October 1952:

René Magritte, *Personal Values*, 1952, oil on canvas.

'It is a picture which has been painted quickly and the colours of which (the bedroom, the walls, the shaving gear and the glass) make me feel sick, I am so depressed that I cannot yet get used to it . . . Be an angel and explain it to me.'[8] On 24 October Magritte riposted:

> from the point of view of immediate usefulness, of what
> relevance is the notion that, for instance, a sky is chasing
> around the walls of a bedroom or a gigantic match lying on
> the carpet or an enormous comb standing upright on the bed?
> . . . In my picture, the comb . . . has specifically lost its 'social
> character', it has become an object of useless luxury, which may,
> as you say, leave the spectator feeling helpless or even make
> him ill. Well, this is proof of the effectiveness of the picture.

He concluded, 'Furthermore, all the reasons in the world are powerless to make anyone like anything.'[9]

The walls in *Personal Values* are literally porous – their solidity is replaced with the insubstantiality of air, sky and clouds, while the solid quality is, in *trompe l'oeil* fashion, emphasized by the ceiling's cracks. Such paintings draw our attention to the importance of Magritte's early experience, before he took up painting professionally, when he worked in the wallpaper factory and learnt how to maximize the illusion potentials of wallpaper. The topsy-turvy universe of *Personal Values* mixes inside and outside and large and small, continuously asserting through its bizarre juxtapositions the constructedness of this environment. The painting's merging of different genres of interior, landscape and still-life also clearly makes use of the potentials of the fairground and the camera obscura to turn the world upside down and invert conventional relations.

The visual friction created by Magritte's mixing of genres is enhanced further by his representing oversized objects in the manner of still-life painting, this arguably being the genre most closely associated with the domestic interior and its symbolization of the ideological interiority associated with bourgeois social spaces. The depictions of objects are reminiscent of typical representations of objects in still-life paintings of Franco-Flemish artists during the seventeenth century, such as Pieter Claesz's *Still-life with Turkey Pie* (1627), in which a centrally situated drinking glass and the coffee pot to its left deceptively distort and reorganize relations between the precisely depicted objects displayed on the table. Traditional generic categories are, in paintings like *Personal Values*, defamiliarized and inverted, and proportions are reversed. The vastness of the sky, the ultimate signifier of sublime exteriority, is transformed into the interior surface of a three-sided room, reminiscent of the dramatic space established by 'fourth-wall' realist theatre. These oversized objects connect to Magritte's developing exploration of the relations between the distinct but connected (and sometimes overlapping) image repertoires of traditional or high art painting and mass-market advertising. While the presentation and finish of his objects allude to Dutch painting, still-life and *trompe l'oeil* traditions, this clearly masculine assemblage of shaving brush, soap, empty glass, matchstick and comb could also derive from an advert for a shaving product, drawing on Magritte's lifelong connection to the advertising industry and his work for interior decorating firms.

The Panoramic 1950s

The fairground also affords insights into aspects of works Magritte made in the 1950s, particularly in relation to his likely having encountered there, as a young boy, the optical device of the panorama. At the turn of the century the fairground was the space where one would encounter technological innovations like automata, the illusionism of wax models and conjurors, and optical and auditory inventions such as the camera obscura, panoramas, dioramas, cosmoramas and phonographs.[10] Like much modernist art, Magritte's work displays the influence of a number of innovative optical devices. The influence of stereoscopy, for example, can be seen in paintings like *The Enchanted Pose* (1927), which shows a double image of a Picassoesque (1917–25), monumental neoclassical nude leaning on a pillar. *Foolhardy* (1925) depicts a double image of a moustachioed, military-uniformed man with his left arm bandaged and in a sling, while in *Portrait of Paul Nougé* (1927) the portrait is doubled but the background varies, as does the jigsaw-patterned fragment of door that Nougé grips. Such uses of stereoscopy as a rhetorical trick afford the painter the opportunity to explore repetition and difference within a single frame (focusing, for example, on the tension between repetition of foreground elements and difference between background ones, also explored in 1935's *Perpetual Motion*), and at the same time to play with allusions to the potentials of perspectival shifting (or the viewer's desire for it) to map the two images onto each other, producing an ideal singularity which the imitated stereoscopic painting nevertheless resists. These experiments with doubling and perception also allude to famous images from art history, such as the anonymous double portrait of *The Cholmondeley Ladies* (*c.* 1600–1610). The modern optical devices that created such new perceptions were frequently showcased as popular attractions at local fairs. However, it is likely that Magritte encountered them in a much larger public arena: the Belgian World's Fairs held during his childhood.

These fairs were significant events in the Magritte household, as is clear from the smaller-scale 1911 Exposition de Charleroi. Open from April to November, the exposition was frequented by hundreds of thousands of visitors and was held to showcase the exceptional achievements of a region at the forefront of the Industrial Revolution, while also exhibiting the artistic and cultural wealth of Hainaut and Wallonia.[11] Magritte would have certainly visited it, given its close proximity to Châtelet, and its many acclaimed attractions included pavilions, a large Luna Park, a waterslide and a scenic railway, cinematic festivals, exhibitions showing Mosan art alongside works by contemporary Belgian painters (such as Joachim Patinier, Jacques Du Broeucq, Jean Del Cour and Félicien Rops), spectacles such as a Spanish village and a Japanese garden, and 'ethnological' displays including real people from different countries. The young Magritte was closely involved in this exposition as his father opened the Magritte house in Châtelet as part of the festival accompanying the fair, and one of Magritte's paintings ('depicting horses in a field'[12]) was displayed on a borrowed easel to visitors to the house. According to Albert Chavepeyer, a painter who had been close to Magritte in his childhood and youth, 'There was a veritable procession of curious visitors. A great many of the townspeople of Châtelet wanted to see the "phenomenon" and his masterpiece.'[13] Thus Magritte and his artwork were strangely positioned in the 1911 Exposition as a fairground spectacle.

In the late nineteenth and early twentieth centuries Belgium hosted four World's Fairs: the 1897 Exposition Internationale de Bruxelles, the Exposition Universelle et Internationale de Liège in 1905 (a second was planned for either 1915 or 1918 but cancelled due to the First World War),[14] the Exposition Universelle et Internationale de Bruxelles in 1910 and the 1913 Exposition Universelle et Internationale in Ghent. These were huge projects employing extensive visual fakery and illusion in a vast but temporary artificial setting.[15] They would have made a profound impression on Magritte's artistic eye. These fairs represented Belgium's colonies as well as the country's global trading partners and were a major commercial and entertainment space for the fast-growing European bourgeoisie. Twenty countries were represented in the 1910 Brussels Exposition, which opened on 23 April and attracted over thirteen million international visitors. The Magrittes would have been among them, given Leopold's business interests, the family's wealth and the excitement of twelve-year-old René and his brothers about the vast array of attractions. Its spectacles included a Luna Park (where, as one commentator notes, 'one's most American fantasies are met'[16]), as well as waterslides, rollercoasters, panoramas, photographic exhibitions and displays of the newest cinematic inventions. Colonial displays such as a replica Senegalese village complete with mothers and babies were exhibited alongside paintings by historical Flemish artists like Rubens and recent French Impressionists and post-Impressionists including Renoir, Monet, Bonnard, Signac, Vuillard and Matisse. A contemporary visitor described the exposition:

We are in an old city, but in a city in celebration, in a city where we drink, where we eat, where we dance, in a city that celebrates its guests. Of these, some dine with the

bourgeois or at the inn, others dine at the castle . . . Think
of the thousand amusements that will be found there:
Punch and Judy shows, cinematographs, puppet theatres,
singing cafés, picturesque cabarets, street singers.[17]

Part of the huge cultural attraction of this artificial
environment was its ability to present reproductions scaled for
mass consumption, using optical technologies such as dioramas,
panoramas and film showings to create in enclosed spaces realistic
external views in seeming full size, or miniature exoticized
elsewheres such as foreign cities or colonial villages. Sweeping
dioramas and panoramic views were carefully painted, taking
full advantage of modern understandings of perception and the
deceptive potentials of *trompe l'oeil* and other visual tricks. These
spectacular media achieved specific effects and illusions – bringing
the outside in, or transposing the foreign and exotic into the
home country. The Brussels fair, for example, included elaborate
feather and flower dioramas in its French pavilion, and the 1913
Ghent Exposition catalogue listed attractions including dioramas
of famous battles – 'diorama's die het leven in Congo weergeven'
(dioramas depicting life in the Congo) and 'weidse, verklarende
diorama's over de katoenteelt' (extensive explanatory dioramas of
cotton cultivation).[18]

Since the early nineteenth century, panoramas had offered
another extremely popular spectacle in Europe and the United
States, creating the frisson of seeing vast vistas without having to
travel and in full knowledge of being in an enclosed environment.
They continued to offer a significant attraction at World's Fairs
in the early twentieth century (the 1905 Exposition, for example,
showed a panorama of medieval Liège), and again the spectacle
they presented would have captured Magritte's artistic attention
and imagination.[19] Panoramas were large painted and staged
scenes, carefully lit and displayed in purpose-built spaces to convey

an immersive experience to the viewer, as if the sceneries before their eyes were real. They fulfilled the dual roles of spectacular entertainment and (usually ideologically imbued) didactic purposes.

The young Magritte may well also have experienced a panorama at the very successful Théâtre Mécanique Morieux. Touring across Belgium, and being a returning annual attraction of fairs such as that held in Charleroi in August, this was a *theatrum mundi*, a mechanical theatre whose success rested on huge dioramas, moving panoramas, cyclorama paintings and marionettes. A *Gazette de Charleroi* article from 6 August 1908 describes the Morieux theatre as one of the annual fair's most extraordinary attractions, its programme ranging from mechanical acrobatic automata to a gigantic diorama showing 'Captain Wellmann's Expedition to the North Pole, with all the adventures of wintering in the ice'.[20] The article continues (making the theatre sound like the IMAX of its day): 'And now what about the Imperator-Bio? Its splendid views take place every evening on a screen of 100 square metres, with absolute fixity, a beautiful clarity and incomparable relief.'[21] Similarly, a 1910 article in the Liège newspaper *La Meuse* narrates a Morieux theatre visit by 350 children at a Brussels fair: 'The various pictures that they were given to see (wintering in the ice, naval combat, hunting lions, a depiction of the climax of the adventures of Siegfried) are an admirable object lesson presented with a real artistic concern.'[22] Magritte would have also certainly known the Morieux theatre and its optical attractions from early childhood, as it visited Châtelet. An article in the *Journal de Charleroi* of 19 November 1905 (Magritte being eight at the time) announced the programme of the Morieux theatre and its 'original *Cinématographe parlant*' (speaking cinematograph) as consisting of: 'Exposition de Paris [another World's Fair], Russian–Japanese War, Automatons, Apotheosis, etc.' The show finished with the cinematograph showing: 'Napoleon, The Passion, The Life of a

Player, The Omers, etc.'[23] Another panorama of which Magritte would have been aware at least later in his life (and which can still be seen today) is that completed in 1881 by Hendrik Willem Mesdag in The Hague, of a painted seascape enhanced by staged props that generate the spatial, rather than simply pictorial, illusion of three-dimensionality.

Unlike the upper-class appeal of panel painting, the panorama attracted and entertained a mass audience. Despite often being condemned by artists, the panorama triggered a 'panoramic consciousness' in nineteenth-century painting, evident in works like Caspar David Friedrich's *Moonrise over the Sea* (1821), which shows two men walking out onto the rocks that extend into the sea 'so they can experience the thrill of being virtually encircled by the vast "panoramic" horizon line'.[24] Magritte seems to have borrowed these two men and reclothed them in coats and bowler hats – the conventional dress of the bourgeois Belgian gentleman – as a very similar pair of small, dark figures, one with a stick. Indeed, these figures start to appear in various of his paintings from the 1950s onwards, establishing these images as extensions of Friedrich's Romantic panoramic consciousness restated in Magritte's painted modernist enigmas. As in Friedrich's painting, we see Magritte's characters only from behind: their repeated insertion into different images, cut-and-pasted from one context to another as recurrent embodiments of a kind of leisurely modernist voyeurism, suggests an extended analysis of the act of looking. Their constitution as a couple suggests another version of the stereoscopic pairs discussed earlier, but they seem also to belong to the modern archetype of the pair to be found in characters like Vladimir and Estragon in Samuel Beckett's play *Waiting for Godot* (first performed in 1953), a pair that draws in turn on cinematic couples like Laurel and Hardy.

Magritte's pair first appear in his 1950 painting *The Horizon*, a title that establishes immediately the figures' close relation to Friedrich's painting and the 'panoramic consciousness' it reveals. The two small figures are here painted on what appears (in relation to them) to be a huge plank of wood stuck in a sandy beach, behind which is depicted a seascape. They are next seen in *The Art of Conversation* (1950), a landscape in which their smallness is emphasized by a gigantic rock formation dominating the vista. They form a group of letters which can be read as *Rêve* (Dream), *Crève* (Chill or Death) and *Trêve* (Truce). More closely examined, the letters also seem to name the Surrealist writer René Crevel (1900–1935). This painting is part of Magritte's lifelong dialogue with Bretonian notions of dreams and their penetrability – here the dream, which (Freud argued) offered the '*via regia*' to the unconscious with which Bretonian Surrealism was so concerned, is represented by immobile stones which seem to constitute written words.[25] These invite (but also resist) conventional readerly interpretation, offering in return permutations of key Surrealist words, suggesting that, in Magritte's critique of Breton, the unconscious merely reveals whatever it is that one seeks within it.

Magritte's pair of voyeurs tend to be found perusing classically panoramic vistas, open spaces with vast horizons. In a version of *The Art of Conversation* painted around 1963 they are placed floating in a cloudy, Turneresque sky over a Romantic landscape complete with winding river. In *The World Awake* (also *c.* 1963), the figures are dwarfed by a stone sphere placed in a seascape, and framed by huge manifestations resembling three stone curtains (petrified versions of the theatrical curtains of earlier works, and forms recurring in paintings like *The Heart of Love* of 1960, another variation on Magritte's stereoscope experiments). The objects and curtains emphasize the staged character of this panoramic vista evoking the static, sculpturally monumental qualities of large panoramic visions and the sublime effects resulting from the combination of size and the viewer's awareness of the scene's evident artifice. While

René Magritte, *The Art of Conversation*, 1950, oil on canvas.

these late paintings are relatively small, their sublime effects are achieved through the differentials of scale effected by their content.

The pair of figures appear again in *Portrait of Stéphy Langui* (1961), here observing a panoramic seascape, gazing out through a huge archway from a seemingly gigantic interior. A large stone beside them emphasizes the scene's monumentality, while an immense female head (the portrait of the painting's title) peers back at them from above. This painting clearly adapts a still from a 1939 Paramount Pictures animation by Dave Fleischer of Jonathan Swift's *Gulliver's Travels*.[26] Friedrich's signifiers of the Romantic sublime are here mashed up with the mass-cultural iconography of a cinematic cartoon, producing an image whose effects marry dimensions of both – Romantic sublimity is ironically undercut by Magritte's adaptation of modern Hollywood iconography, while the cartoon image is reversed and inverted, transformed from the smiling male head of Gulliver to a blank-faced female head, with

Magritte's two figures replacing the comically cowering Lilliputians of the cartoon. The overall effect is one of ironic displacement, the 'high seriousness' characteristic of Magritte's wandering voyeurs counterpointing the absurdity of Swift's satirical exaggerations and their cartoon cinematic rendering. Indeed, the effect of exaggeration through juxtaposition is revealed, in this direct allusion to it, as the obvious trope employed by Magritte in all these paintings.

Such works perform an extended critique, via a deconstruction of panoramic vision, of Bretonian Surrealism's pretensions to represent the sublime depths of the unconscious. Locating sublimity in satirical versions of the Romantic landscapes of Friedrich, Magritte constantly reveals (through the insistent presence of the two viewing men, metonyms of the audience that both sees the scene and consumes its meanings) the artifice of such views and the necessary fact that human perception intervenes between the viewed spectacle and the viewing subject. These pictures relocate the viewer of the sublime natural moment, with all its connotations of divine totality of perception, within the frame of the image, while the evident artifice of immensely oversized, constructed monuments, stone curtains and other recurrent elements expresses Magritte's constant exposure of something exceeding or outside the sublime totality. Through the insertion of his viewing men, Magritte undercuts sublime pretensions. As such, each painting becomes part of a sequence, its individual, panoramic gesture towards completeness perpetually undermined by the existence of other versions indicating its incompleteness.

In these pictures Magritte is engaged in exposing the artifice of conventional panoramic views. Where photographic panoramas worked hard to efface the joins between the frames, Magritte resists this effacement, representing the panoramic illusion while also revealing its constructedness.[27] This is clear in the important 1960 painting *The Memoirs of a Saint*, in which a curved curtain creates a circular, contained, empty space reminiscent of the circus ring, with the section nearest the viewer left open. The curtain stands in a bare, dark interior, which clearly evokes a space that we might call cinematic. The inside surface of the curtain displays a seascape dominated by a Magrittean blue sky with white clouds – a vision of light amid the gloom of the image. Sylvester notes that this painting derives from a print 'published in *La Nature* in 1896, which shows one of the photographic panoramas of the period – the American invention called the "cyclorama"' which allowed 'faithful representation of the phenomena of movement and life, as well as of inanimate views and landscapes'.[28] The cyclorama is a specific form of enclosed panorama, affording the contained viewer a 360-degree vista and simultaneously locating the viewer at the centre of the perceived reality. In this painting Magritte exploits the 'iconic shape of the panorama rotunda', a device which, as Alison Griffiths notes, was highly successful in creating 'a heightened sensation of moving out of the immediate and into the hyper-real'.[29] Rather than immersing the viewer in the panoramic vision, though, Magritte positions them outside of it, exposing its constructedness.

Magritte's explorations of the possibilities of 'panoramic vision' continued in the mural works which he was commissioned to produce from the 1950s. These commissions enabled Magritte to insert his image repertoire directly into theatrical spaces, reinforcing the connections between his paintings and the worlds of staged representations. He was awarded them partly on the basis of his increasing exhibition prominence during the early 1950s, which was establishing him as a major figure in modern art. In 1951 he was commissioned to paint the ceiling decoration of the Théâtre Royal des Galeries in Brussels, an invitation that coincided with his second exhibition at Alexander Iolas's Hugo Gallery in New York. The Théâtre Royal des Galeries, originally a casino, was converted in 1900 into a theatre, hosting (as the 1920 *Guide bleu* to Belgium

René Magritte, *The Memoirs of a Saint*, 1960, oil on canvas.

notes) comedy, vaudeville, comic operas and operettas, and revues. The building underwent a complete reconstruction in 1951, and Magritte's contribution was to be the spectacular centrepiece of the renovated theatre auditorium.[30] His original fresco design consisted of a circular skyscape of clouds. It initially included *grelots*, the characteristic spherical, bell-like objects that appear in many of his paintings, but the venue owners objected to what they saw as 'obscure symbols', and he was required to remove them.[31] (Later a large chandelier comprising numerous glass balls was hung at the centre of the fresco, compensating for this omission.) The remaining sky picture covers the theatre's ceiling, complementing the panoramic backdrops and scenery of the plays staged below, questioning the relations between interior and exterior, and offering a kind of performance of illusion to parallel the dramatic action.

Two years later, in 1953, Magritte was commissioned to paint a mural for the Casino Communal de Knokke – his first retrospective had been held there in 1952, organized by E.L.T. Mesens, and had run alongside an exhibition of works by another Belgian Surrealist painter, Paul Delvaux (1897–1994). Mesens, returning from London after the closure of the London Gallery in July 1950, was looking for new opportunities in Belgium. His old friend and employer P.-G. Van Hecke introduced him to Gustave Nellens, the owner of the Casino Communal at Knokke, giving him the opportunity to organize significant exhibitions there and at Nellens's nearby hotel, La Réserve. Mesens organized several exhibitions in Knokke between 1950 and 1953, including major shows of Picasso, Ernst and Matisse, and a survey exhibition of twentieth-century art. At this time Mesens owned by far the largest collection of works by Magritte, mostly stored at the Palais des Beaux-Arts, and he was keen to raise its value by showing Magritte's work in exhibitions – these included a show in November 1953 at the Lefevre Gallery in London, one of his 'word paintings' at New York's Sidney Janis Gallery in 1954 and, in the same year, Magritte's first major retrospective, at the Palais des Beaux-Arts in Brussels. This show marked the thirtieth anniversary of the publication of Breton's first *Manifesto of Surrealism* and was the first at the Palais to devote such a large amount of space to a Surrealist. The show firmly established Magritte as a leading artist in Belgium.[32]

Following the 1952 retrospective Nellens commissioned Magritte in April 1953 to decorate the Casino Communal's Salle du Lustre (Chandelier Room) with a 'panoramic mural,' the '*Panorama Surréaliste*'.[33] Magritte produced eight oil paintings featuring different elements of the now-conventional Magritte pictorial lexicon. These were then realized on the walls by a team of painters working under his supervision. Staying at the Villa Jaky-Jean, 24 rue de l'Yser in Knokke, with Georgette and their dog Loulou, Magritte described in a letter to his close friends the couple Louis

Scutenaire and Irène Hamoir the happenings of the past week around the production of the mural:

> Dear Stay-at-homes,
> So we have been here – since Monday – Telegraphic style:
> Monday – rain – settling in – row with the landlord's
> wife – extreme fatigue – short-circuit in the evening
> – consequent anxiety – bad night – Supervising the work –
> Tuesday – rain – think of turning on the central heating –
> we feel warmer – Supervision of the work at the Casino –
> Wednesday – not so much rain – met Horeman – painter
> – Journalist – man of steel – pantheist – takes a cold
> bath every morning – ½ hour of exercises – he is in rude
> health – Supervision of the work – Thursday – Sunshine
> – Supervision of the work – Met a bearded young man
> who is studying philology, a friend of Sasson and Van
> Loock, surrealist painter as well for the last four years –
> On the whole, the work at the Casino is 50% satisfactory.
> I have found a method: I ask as much as possible from the
> workmen, but I take care not to demand the impossible –
> All this effort of painting on a gigantic scale has left me
> dazed. I am gradually recovering my usual elasticity
> – perhaps by the time of your proposed visit I shall be
> able to welcome you in a relaxed frame of mind.[34]

Magritte's panoramic mural encircles the Salle du Lustre. Divided by pilasters, its effect is enhanced by the curved walls and corners to resemble a cyclorama, with the viewer contained within and positioned at the centre of the spectacle. Magritte's paintings offer cloud-, sea- and landscapes, evoking the typical panoramic themes evident in (for example) Mesdag's panorama in The Hague. Magritte is again playing with inside–outside relations by bringing into the building the sea, sky and landscapes whose real counterparts could be seen outside the casino (which was built directly overlooking the sea). The eight distinct sections incorporate into these panoramic views a kind of 'retrospective' of Magritte's works, representing key images and themes from his career to date, such as the houses of *The Empire of Light* (which exists in three versions all dating from the early 1950s) and his self-portrait as a hatted and cloaked birdcage in *The Healer* (the earliest version of which dates from 1937). The artifice of the panoramic illusion is thus emphasized by the inclusion of recognizable elements from what is by now a well-known painterly oeuvre, and Magritte also structured his eight panels to accommodate the architectural and decorative features of the Salle du Lustre, making them elements of the installation that both reinforce and expose its illusory effects. The inauguration of Magritte's contribution to the Salle was accompanied by the opening of Mesens's large Max Ernst exhibition and was part of the spectacular sixth Belgian Summer Festival (July–August 1953), which included a film festival in Knokke that drew stars such as Yves Montand, Maurice Chevalier and Juliette Gréco to the town.

Another of Magritte's large-scale panoramic works was a 1956 mural for the Salle des Congrès (Congress Hall) of the Palais des Beaux-Arts in Charleroi. The building itself is situated at the place du Manège and was built in 1935 on the site of the Théâtre des Variétés, which hosted a number of contemporary theatrical and cinema stars. The Palais would have been intimately familiar to Magritte, and the Théâtre des Variétés was, before its post-First World War transformation in 1928 by Gustave Bernard, the host site of Auguste Bovyn's famous circus, the formative influence of which on Magritte was described earlier. Appropriately, given the significance of the stage discussed here, the commission required Magritte 'to execute a mural painting, approximately 16 m × 2.30 m, on the frieze above the stage in the Salle des Congrès of the Palais des Beaux-Arts in Charleroi'.[35] The stage itself, with its ruffled curtains, light-coloured columns and rectangular apron, recalls Magritte's *Lost Jockey* paintings discussed earlier (and, as if on cue, the lost jockey enters this mural from the right). The mural offers a panoramic perspective, looking outwards on to landscapes, while the topic of this panorama is again a retrospective of Magritte's iconic images, now recycled in a more obviously surrealistic landscape format. As Magritte himself comments frustratedly: 'The Charleroi architect will be accepting the frieze willy-nilly, because he thinks I have "invented nothing"; according to him everything to be seen in my study is already known: bird, sky, house, etc. . . . are banalities devoid of interest.'[36]

These large-scale commissions represented a late-career compromise on Magritte's part between the opportunity to make fairly conventional art that makes money, and the critically subversive intentions of his earlier work. The analytical illusionism of his camera-obscura-influenced works of the 1930s gives way to the more accessible public staging of his work as spectacle in the panoramic murals of the 1950s – but this journey from subversion to conventionality takes place via a series of strange detours and challenging connections. Magritte's allegiances throughout his career can be seen as different ways of negotiating the tension between bourgeois conventionality and its subversion, and the next chapter explores some of Magritte's connections throughout the 1930s and 1940s with more eccentric political and avant-garde positions.

5

Subversive Allegiances

Magritte's painterly interrogation through the 1930s and '40s of
the forms and illusions of bourgeois realism paralleled the complex
relationship between Surrealism and communism, and his own
problematic relations to the party. Magritte seems to have joined
the Parti Communiste de Belgique (PCB) three times, in 1932, 1936
and 1945. While he had an on-and-off relationship with the party
as such, his series of positions on the dangers of bourgeois values
and the need for liberation from them can be tracked throughout
his career. In a 1945 letter to the PCB he wrote: 'The only way
that poets and painters can fight against the bourgeois economy
is to give their works precisely that content which challenges
the bourgeois ideological values propping up the bourgeois
economy.'[1]

The Surrealist group in Brussels, including Paul Nougé, a
founding member of the PCB, was by the late 1920s heavily involved
in debates within international Surrealism about communism.
These debates led to particularly strong disputes between the
Parisian Surrealists, several of whom joined the party. Others
quickly realized that the party's conception of art and how it
could serve communist ideals – that is, its preference for a realist
'proletarian' art – differed significantly from the kinds of aesthetic
and political liberation desired by Surrealism. The deterioration
of the relationship between the international Surrealists and
communism is evident from the 1935 declaration 'On the Time the

Le Rendez-vous de chasse, Brussels, 1934. Seated (L–R): Irène Hamoir, Marthe Beauvoisin, Georgette Magritte; standing (L–R): E.L.T. Mesens, René Magritte, Louis Scutenaire, André Souris, Paul Nougé.

Surrealists were Right', signed by French and Belgian Surrealists in opposition to the rise of Stalinist authoritarianism. While this meant a significant break between the French Surrealists and the Parti Communiste Français (PCF), communism remained significant in Magritte's thought in the late 1930s. It features prominently in his November 1938 lecture 'Lifeline 1'. The lecture addresses 'Ladies and Gentlemen, Comrades' and aligns itself explicitly with communist ideals, stating that the people 'on whose side I am proud to be, despite the utopian attitude they are taxed with, consciously crave the proletarian revolution which will change the world'.[2] He goes on to recall the period around 1925 when he met with Nougé, Mesens and Scutenaire:

> We were drawn together by common concerns. We met the [Parisian] Surrealists who were violently demonstrating

their disgust of bourgeois society. Their revolutionary claims being ours, we joined them in the service of the proletarian revolution. It was a great failure. The politicians who lead workers' parties were, in fact, far too egotistical and short-sighted to take the Surrealists' contributions into account. They were the high-and-mighty men who were permitted to compromise seriously the cause of the proletariat in 1914. All kinds of baseness and treachery were allowed. In Germany, when they represented a mass of perfectly disciplined workers and could have used that power to crush that bloody nuisance, Hitler, they simply gave in to him and his handful of fanatics.[3]

Magritte's continued Marxist critiques of the bourgeoisie and of capitalism, and his alignment of the artist with the worker, can also be seen in his article 'Bourgeois Art', written in collaboration with Scutenaire and published in the British Surrealist journal *London Bulletin* in March 1939:

People do not want a diamond for its intrinsic properties – its authentic qualities alone – but because, as it costs a great deal, it gives the man who possesses it a kind of superiority over his fellow men, and is a concrete expression of social inequality. Besides, things have become so absurd that if you buy a fake diamond unawares, you will be just as satisfied, because you have paid the price of the genuine article. It is no different with art. Capitalist hypocrisy, always refusing to take a thing for what it is, attributes to art the characteristics of a superior activity, quite different from the activities of the average man.[4]

This commitment to Marxism on the brink of the war continued after its end. On 8 September 1945, *Le Drapeau rouge* (The Red Flag), the party's newsletter, announced Magritte's (re)joining in a front-page article accompanied by a large photograph. Despite this ostensibly ideological continuity Georgette assigned Magritte's post-war return to the party less to philosophical reasons than to a sense of gratitude (widely felt in newly liberated Belgium) towards the Russians.[5] The Belgian Surrealists also hoped to influence the PCB's attitudes on art and culture from the inside (Nougé and Magritte also joined the PCB's art society with this aim).[6]

On 12 January 1946 Magritte donated a version of *The Memory* to a tombola organized as part of the 'Oeuvres offertes par l'Amicale des Arts plastiques' (Works offered to the Association of Plastic Arts), which had opened on 4 January at the Galerie L'Ecrin d'Art. He also attended PCB meetings with friends from different artistic groupings from Brussels, Antwerp and Hainaut, including Nougé, Colinet, Scutenaire, Hamoir, Mariën, Lefrancq and Pol Bury. Nevertheless, the gap between the PCB's rather utilitarian understanding of art and Magritte and Nougé's position on Surrealism as supportive of communism proved unbridgeable. Magritte realized that the communists' admiration for past painters and conventional awe before the value of the unique work of art meant that they essentially shared the uncritical bourgeois esteem of art he aimed to critique. As he notes in his 1938 lecture:

The subversive aspect of Surrealism obviously worried the traditional workers' politicians, who are at times indistinguishable from the most strenuous defenders of the bourgeois world. Surrealist thought is revolutionary on all levels and is, of necessity, opposed to the bourgeois conception of art. It so happens that left-wing politicians agree with that bourgeois conception and, when it comes to painting, they don't want to tough it out unless it toes the line. However, the politician who calls himself a revolutionary and who must therefore look to the future, ought to be opposed to the bourgeois conception of art, because it consists of a cult uniquely devoted to the works of the past and a desire to impede the progress of art.[7]

That relations were brittle between the communists and the Belgian Surrealists is further made clear in a letter Magritte wrote in 1947 in which he notes that the artists were 'greeted with hostility and distrust on the part of the Communist Party', and complains that the communist press was ignoring Belgian Surrealist efforts: 'not a word in *Le Drapeau rouge* about the works of Nougé, Scutenaire, Mariën and Magritte which were sent to them'.[8] Party distrust of and puzzlement over Surrealism can be traced in reviews by Bob Claessens in *Le Drapeau rouge* of the 'Exhibition of Belgian and Foreign Masters: Painting, Sculpture, Craft', which opened on 11 October 1947 at the House of the Communist Press in Brussels. Reviews published on 15 and 22 October 1947 describe 'Breton and his gang' as sell-outs to 'Wall Street bankers', referring to French Surrealist activity in America during the Second World War. Claessens nevertheless concludes:

> Their works have no place with us. But some of the surrealists have recognized that the enemy was societal and that it was restricted to the capitalist society of our times. They understood that one needs to lead an organized fight against it, and have joined our ranks. In their works they conduct experiments, which they call scientific, on the shock-effect which is brought forth by unexpected juxtapositions of form and colour which can be triggered by a familiar object, removed from its usual environment and presented in a new context. For these 'revolutionary surrealists' we reserved a wall on our first floor.[9]

Magritte's letter in 1947 was not just concerned with this disrespect for the Belgian Surrealists. He also criticized curatorial decisions in this exhibition, particularly the inclusion of James Ensor, who 'showed his paintings in Germany during the Occupation', and of 'other "stars" sanctioned by the bourgeoisie', accusing the Communist Party of complying with bourgeois ideology that values 'artists who are dead' over the ones who are alive. The letter concludes with the withdrawal of Magritte and others from the PCB's upcoming Antwerp Conference in November 1947, 'whose absurd theme is the search for ways for the artist to participate in political agitation'.[10]

Magritte also wrote to CPD members about the hypocritical coverage in the 22 October 1947 issue of *Le Drapeau rouge* of the Belgian queen's visit to the exhibition, which noted that she arrived in a 'stylish Buick': 'It is damaging to show communist artists and visitors arranged in a half-circle around the queen and to make an outstanding free advertisement for a car brand.'[11] Marcel Mariën, with whom Magritte had a complex, on–off friendship, published this letter in the journal *Les Lèvres nues* in September 1970, three years after Magritte's death, adding a photograph showing Georgette 'chatting about painting' with Queen Fabiola at an exhibition at the Galerie Brachot in Brussels in January 1968.[12]

Magritte eventually lost patience with the PCB. He complained to Patrick Waldberg of attending party meetings, being asked to design posters and having all his designs rejected. After a few months he stopped going – 'there was no expulsion or break, but from my side a complete alienation, an ultimate distancing.'[13] Mariën's critique of Magritte's apparent political hypocrisy highlights the complex and sometimes compromised relations between the latter's left-wing and sometimes communist politics and his reliance on the art market and commercial artistic practice. Magritte's growing prosperity and fame during the 1950s (evident in commissions such as that from the Belgian government in 1958 to paint a mural for the new Palais des Congrès in Brussels) increasingly alienated him from his Brussels friends. Paul Nougé sarcastically noted of his purchase of a grand piano that it was fine to have one but useful to know how to play it. Mesens noticed that the Saturday evening gatherings at the Magrittes' became increasingly an opportunity for Magritte to glean flattery from young admirers, who hung on his every word while he behaved as if he were a 'master'.

Marcel Mariën and Post-war Belgian Surrealism

Marcel Mariën, author of the first monograph on Magritte in 1943, became perhaps the artist's most vocal critic, even after his death in 1967. Mariën, who worked across poetry, photography, object- and film-making, and collage, represented a new generation of Belgian Surrealist artists. Born in Antwerp in 1920 and mainly based there throughout his life, he first encountered Magritte's paintings in a 1937 exhibition and travelled to Brussels to meet the older artist. Very quickly he forged a close relationship with Magritte and the Surrealist group in Brussels, soon exhibiting together with the others in the 'Surrealist Objects and Poems' exhibition organized by Mesens in November 1937 at the London Gallery. Mariën oversaw posthumous publications such as Magritte's texts from the period 1946–50, which appeared in 1972 in *Manifestes et autres écrits* (Manifestos and Other Writings).

He claimed in his autobiography, *Le Radeau de la mémoire* (The Raft of Memory; 1983), to have worked with Magritte to perform elaborate pranks and forgeries, notably in connection with the 1943 monograph, for which, Mariën states, Magritte urgently needed money to pay for image rights.[14] Despite the artist's appalling financial situation at this time, the book appeared with all reproductions in colour, and Magritte never explained where the money came from. Based on the citation of postcards and letters allegedly written between Mariën and Magritte from 1937 to 1962 (later published in 1977 as *La Destination*), Mariën claims the money came from the sale of forged artworks created by Magritte – imitations of Picasso, Braque, De Chirico, Klee, Titian and Ernst.

These letters are of questionable provenance, and the reliability of Mariën's narratives is further complicated by several images assigned in his publications to Magritte, which seem actually to have been forged by himself.[15] This also makes the wider reliability of Mariën's documentation of Belgian Surrealism problematic – his Surrealist games and activities are, indeed, comparable in their subversive potentials to the deceptions of Fantômas.

Perhaps the most momentous instance of Mariën's forgery was the spoof advertisement of a Grande Baisse from 1962, another satirical subversion of bourgeois values. It was produced by Mariën but ascribed to Magritte. The flyer, announcing a 'Great Bargain Sale' of Magritte's artworks, was sent to the opening of Magritte's retrospective at the Casino in Knokke, falsely naming the Belgian poet André Bosmans's journal *Rhétorique* (which published many Magritte drawings) as its origin and forging the journal's stamp. The letter was headed by a caption showing a one-hundred-franc banknote with Leopold I's head replaced by Magritte's. The title that appeared below this, *Les travaux forcés*, cites the warning printed on Belgian banknotes – 'La loi punit le contrefacteur des travaux forcés' (The punishment for counterfeiting is hard labour).[16] Under Belgian law the reproduction of a current banknote in any form constitutes forgery unless it is overprinted with the word 'specimen'. This photomontage, clearly attributed to Magritte – possibly another double bluff in which not only the banknote is forged, but also the forger himself – led the director of the Belgian National Bank to call in the police, who immediately phoned Magritte. Mariën's stunt was remarkably successful – the affair extended to Paris and involved Breton anonymously publishing an article in *Combat* on 3 July 1962 that, not recognizing the forgery, praised Magritte's humour in the Grande Baisse leaflet.

Leo Dohmen, a photographer and art dealer and Mariën's accomplice, claimed that, following Mariën's suggestion, he was the actual producer of the photomontage. According to Dohmen, the image and its title, *Les travaux forcés*, were deliberate allusions on Mariën's part to another, much more serious forgery, namely five hundred counterfeit hundred-franc banknotes allegedly made by Magritte and his brother Paul in 1953, which Mariën had helped to distribute. Highlighting Magritte's apparent commercialism, which he had himself often criticized in his communications with the PCB in the 1930s and '40s, the Grande Baisse advert mocked Magritte's purchase of a fur coat, jewels and an expensive car for Georgette, parodying Magritte in saying: 'my painting is coming to resemble a form of merchandise . . . People now buy my paintings as they buy land, a fur coat or jewels.'[17]

The Belgian Surrealists regularly met at the bistro La Fleur en Papier Doré, which belonged to the gallerist and art dealer Geert van Bruane. While Magritte's friendships with Lecomte, Hamoir, Scutenaire and Goemans continued into the 1950s, and new ones were established with a younger generation of poets and artists such as André Bosmans, Jacques Wergifosse, Rachel Baes and Jane Graverol, his close associates Mariën, Mesens and Nougé felt increasingly estranged. They were particularly opposed to his commercialism in working to order to 'supply copies of his most famous pictures, when he had always detested painting as [merely] a manual occupation and used to say that, if he became rich, he would no longer paint anything but the very few pictures he was really keen on'.[18] In one instance he painted 53 paintings during 1956 and 1957 for the Chicago lawyer Barnet Hodes, all replicas of older works, each measuring around 23 × 17 centimetres (9 × 7 in.). It was a kind of evolution of what he had done for the first Levy Gallery exhibition in 1936. Hodes wanted to create a 'Magritte wall' in one room of his home to form (as he noted in a letter to Magritte of 29 January 1957) a 'representative collection of your wonderful pictures in the small form that I enjoy so much'.[19]

Magritte felt deeply compromised by these requirements, a frustration clear from a letter to Hodes from 8 April 1960:

Belgian Surrealists in front of the café La Fleur en Papier Doré (55 rue des Alexiens, Brussels), photograph, 8 March 1953. (L–R) Marcel Mariën, Albert van Loock, Camille Goemans, Georgette Magritte, Geert van Bruane, Louis Scutenaire, E.L.T. Mesens, René Magritte and Paul Colinet.

As regards my next works, I must tell you that it is becoming difficult for me to re-do copies of works which are already old. I need to be able to create variants that bring a new youth to old ideas. I cannot force my 'inspiration' in this way, as I am preoccupied with finding new ideas for paintings. It is obvious that if I always make replicas of the same painting, I might think that there is nothing else for me to paint.[20]

And yet Magritte's 'reproduction' of his own works, a kind of self-forgery, strangely blends his apparent commercialism with his political urge to critique and subvert the bourgeois valorization of artistic uniqueness, originality and mastery – all elements perpetuating the capitalist art market. Nevertheless, that Magritte was troubled by the contradictions emerging from his artistic success was clear to those who knew him; his closest friend, Louis Scutenaire, confided in Sylvester that:

> In my opinion – but I might be wrong – success gave Magritte a guilt complex, because in his heart of hearts he was unhappy . . . He was much less agreeable than when he was poor, less warm, less happy with himself.[21]

Nonetheless, Magritte continued throughout his career to collaborate productively with other Belgian Surrealist artists and writers, contributing to their collective activities which were particularly focused on publications. *L'Invention collective*, the first issue of which was published in February 1940, included collaborations between the photographer Raoul Ubac (as publication director) and Magritte as artistic director. Later collaborative activities drew in a new generation of artists. *Le Ciel bleu*, with the subtitle *De l'autre côté du miroir* (The Blue Sky: On the Other Side of the Mirror), published its first issue in February 1945. Reproduced in the middle of the front page was Lewis Carroll's 1871 poem 'The Walrus and the Carpenter', alongside an 'Editorial' including quotes from Erik Satie, Paul Valéry and William Blake, continuing the musical and poetic lineage asserted since the beginnings of the Brussels group. Contributions included the old guard – Hamoir, Colinet, Magritte and Scutenaire – with Breton and Picasso writing on 'Raymond Roussel, le poète extrême'; and works by a new generation that included Mariën and the Belgian painter and poet Christian Dotremont (1922–1979). (The latter was a key figure in post-war Belgian avant-gardes, being a founding member of both the international Revolutionary Surrealist Group in 1946 and, with the Danish artist Asger Jorn, of the COBRA

(Copenhagen–Brussels–Amsterdam) Group of experimental artists in 1948.) The 8 March 1945 issue of *Le Ciel bleu* featured on its front page Magritte's *Le Météore* (1944), a Renoir-period painting showing a horse's head with flowing mane and a forest in the background, and included a major article on Magritte by Mariën. A slightly younger generation of artists close to Magritte included the poet Jacques Wergifosse (1928–2013), who contributed some line drawings of a young girl to the 29 March issue, alongside Magritte's 'Lignes magiques' (Magic Lines) written in response to these.

Another significant moment in the collective history of the Brussels Surrealists was the publication in March 1950 of an eight-page booklet of essays by Colinet, Magritte, Nougé, Mariën and Scutenaire on the subject of the 'cork'. In 1952 Magritte founded the review *La Carte d'après nature*, which appeared in postcard form or as small booklets up to April 1956. Jean Paulhan joked that it was the smallest review in the world – nevertheless it significantly revived Belgian Surrealist activities, featuring work by Magritte's friends such as Colinet, Scutenaire, Hamoir, Lecomte, Mariën and Mesens. Magritte also included non-Surrealist contributors, such as the pharmacist Willy van Hove and the Brussels businessman Justin Rakofsky, whom Magritte had met in 1952 or '53 at a café in the rue Henri Maus where he regularly played chess. He considered soliciting the collaboration of Martin Heidegger, whose work he had probably been familiar with since the early 1930s (Magritte owned several works by Heidegger, particularly from the late 1940s and '50s, and a few secondary sources on modern metaphysics by philosophers such as the Frenchman Jean Wahl and the Belgian Alphonse de Waelhens, who introduced works by Heidegger and Maurice Merleau-Ponty to the Belgian intelligentsia).[22] In 1954 Magritte had an extensive exchange of letters on Heidegger with Alphonse de Waelhens, hoping that De Waelhens would help with any Heidegger translations for *La Carte d'après nature*.

In March 1957 Magritte was elected to the Académie Picard, which had been founded in 1901 in opposition to the official Académie Royale de Belgique. In his acceptance letter he meditated on how 'so called "fantastic art" . . . purports to be truer than the world itself'.[23] Many of Magritte's friends were members, including Victor and the recently retired Pierre Bourgeois (whom Magritte was elected to replace), Paul Delvaux and Lecomte, but there was one person in particular with whom he liked to associate in the Académie: 'It has . . . one member who is a *fairly* remarkable person: De Waelhens, prof. of Philosophy at Louvain University, who translated Heidegger.'[24] Despite seemingly feeling out of place in such a prestigious institutional context, Magritte regularly attended the organization's meetings.

Georges Bataille

The place du Manège embodied another little-discussed but significant aspect of Magritte's work in the 1940s, namely the carnivalesque and its manifestations in this oeuvre in relation to the French thinker and novelist Georges Bataille. In 1913 the annual big carnival and Mardi Gras were held in Charleroi, and included a parade, orchestras and a large ball featuring extravagant illuminations. The annual 'foire de Pâques', or Easter fair (at which Magritte and Georgette may have first met), was also held at the square – according to the *Gazette de Charleroi*'s announcement of this fair, its many attractions included stands selling fries, booths hosting 'phénomènes' (freakshow acts, such as somnambulists), shooting, swings, a museum and carousels.[25]

Some of the wilder *phénomènes* of this fair had their own impact on Magritte's works. 'Madame Adriana the Bearded Lady', a photograph of whom was published in the July 1929 issue of Van Hecke's Belgian journal *Variétés*, resembles Magritte's disturbing mash-up of female nude and portrait, *The Rape* (*Le Viol*) from 1945, which alludes to the violence of the (second) German occupation of Belgium.[26] *Variétés* also reproduced a picture of 'Miss Violetta, the Trunk-Woman' (the title of Magritte's painting repeating the first four letters of her stage name). Violetta was born limbless as a result of tetra-amelia syndrome; her act used oral manipulation to perform everyday actions like combing her hair. Female torsos placed on display plinths and tables are a recurrent image throughout Magritte's work. We also find the double-headed woman in *La Loge* as one of the fairground attractions from the 1910s and '20s – in his book on Belgian fairs Philippe Dimbourg reproduces an undated image of a famous act, the sisters Diva and Cora, twins conjoined at the neck and sharing one body. Magritte's many mythical creatures and spectacular figures, from unicorns to sirens, may also derive from this context. However, perhaps the darkest manifestation of the influence of these carnivalesque *phénomènes* can be found in Magritte's 1946 drawings for renegade Surrealist Georges Bataille's *Madame Edwarda*, a narrative he published in 1941 under the pseudonym Pierre Angélique (a name that, literally translated as 'Stone Angels', connotes the petrified flying creatures Magritte depicts in the 1942 painting *The Companions of Fear*).

The paths of Magritte and Bataille probably first crossed in 1929–30, when the latter was editing the journal *Documents*, which ran to fifteen issues, during a major crisis of Surrealist identity and ideological direction. Several members departed from the circle around Breton or had been excommunicated by him after a series of significant theoretical and aesthetic arguments. As we saw earlier, ideological conflicts also developed at this time between many of the Surrealists and the French Communist Party. Breton sent a questionnaire to Surrealism's participators, enquiring about future collaborations. Bataille's response was 'too many fucking idealists', probably marking the beginning of his own move in a

Siamese twins Diva and Cora, undated.

different avant-garde direction, and certainly sealing his alienation from the Breton fold.[27]

Bataille, who worked as a numismatist at the Bibliothèque Nationale, clearly opposed Breton's Surrealism and was sufficiently charismatic and authoritative to attract his own 'disciples'.[28] *Documents* featured photographs from a range of sources, including dissident Surrealist photographers, stock photographs from picture agencies, film stills, publicity shots, photographs of art objects, ethnographic photographs (such as William Seabrook's photographs of rituals of initiation into voodoo) and photographs of popular-cultural artefacts. The journal offered a particularly

René Magritte, illustrations for a 1946 edition of Georges Bataille's *Madame Edwarda*.

ethnographic take on contemporary culture.[29] Described as 'a war machine against received ideas'[30] by another dissident Surrealist, the writer and ethnographer Michel Leiris, who was also its subeditor, *Documents* brought together contributors like André Masson and Joan Miró with ethnographers, art historians, archaeologists and musicologists. It is likely that Magritte would have read Bataille's publications more generally, and *Documents* specifically. He almost certainly read Bataille's short piece 'The Solar Anus', written in 1927, because in 1928 he painted *The Eye of the Mountain*, in which a huge, black, anus-like sun hangs dolefully above a rocky landscape – the painting could almost be an illustration to accompany Bataille's piece. In the same year, Bataille

René Magritte, *The Eye of the Mountain*, 1928, oil on canvas.

wrote his pornographic novel *Story of the Eye*, its title in turn perhaps echoing that of Magritte's painting. André Blavier's edition of Magritte's *Écrits complets* mentions the anti-Bataillean tract 'Nom de Dieu' (Name of God; May 1943), which labelled Bataille an idealist and which Magritte signed (along with other Surrealists who remained in Paris during the war).[31] The book also briefly refers to a letter from February 1961 from Bataille to Magritte, in which Bataille apologizes for using the word 'absurd' in a previous communication to describe the erotic element in Magritte's work. Both entries are omitted from the German translation of *René Magritte: Sämtliche Schriften* and the English *René Magritte: Selected Writings*. The Magritte *catalogues raisonnés* mention Bataille twice, once in the second *catalogue*, in the context of *Madame Edwarda*:

> Albert Van Loock, the bookseller, brother of Elisabeth
> Altenloh and an old army friend of Mariën, commissioned,
> in 1946, he told us, a set of drawings for an edition
> of Bataille's recent novel, *Madame Edwarda*. He paid
> Magritte for the drawings but failed to publish them.[32]

Only three of the six illustrations for *Madame Edwarda* are reproduced in the *catalogue raisonné*. The second mention of Bataille relates to Magritte's painting *The Persian Letters* of 1959, which seems to have been given or sold by Magritte to Bataille and the third *catalogue* also mentions that in 1960 Magritte and Bataille 'had recently been corresponding (probably about the book [Bataille] was planning to write about Magritte)'.[33]

While these entries suggest that, as far as conventional criticism is concerned, Bataille was marginal to Magritte's oeuvre, pieced together they also paint another picture. Magritte certainly knew of Bataille's work from 1943, when he signed the tract against him, and the two men 'became friends' soon afterwards. However, given the closeness of avant-garde circles, the intellectual significance of

Bataille in late 1920s Paris (where Magritte was living at the time) and *Documents* advertising in issues of *Variétés* in 1929, it seems very likely that Magritte knew Bataille's work at that time. The 'Solar Anus' connections traced above suggest the two men were aware of each other during Magritte's stay in Paris from 1927 to 1930. The various mentions of Bataille also show that over the years after 1943 there was further contact – the *Madame Edwarda* illustrations were made in 1946, Magritte gave *The Persian Letter* to Bataille in 1959, and there was some correspondence between the two men in the early 1960s.

Bataille's admiration for Magritte is confirmed by art historian Patrick Waldberg:

> For Bataille – and we heard him express the view upon a number of occasions – Magritte's achievement better than a great many others illustrated what he meant when he spoke of art as 'the creation of a sensitive reality modifying the world in response for the desire for wonders'.[34]

Bataille appreciated Magritte's work to the extent that he intended to write a book on him, as is confirmed in four letters from Bataille from 1961, copies of which are stored in the Magritte archives at the Menil Foundation. This intention might be still more significant given that Bataille was, as indicated in the letters, very ill by this time and indeed died in July 1962. He writes on 26 July 1960:

> Dear Friend, Since we met I feel bad I have to finish a book [the revised edition of *Guilty*] urgently. In truth it makes me ill. If only you knew how keen I am to work for you . . . Believe me when I say that our encounter is profoundly significant to me.[35]

Bataille's sense of urgency about this project is again evident in a letter of 2 March 1961: 'I can't wait for the moment when I will be able to work on a book the title of which would be your name.'[36]

The 1960–61 letter exchanges also indicate that Bataille was intensely keen to include Magritte's *Olympia* (1948) in his book *The Tears of Eros* (1961). A copy of the book was in Magritte's library at the time of his death, along with one other book by Bataille, volume II of *La Somme atheologique*. Bataille was also keen to include Magritte's 1947 painting *The Sage's Carnival* in *The Tears of Eros*. This work from his 'sunlit' or 'Renoir' period depicts in predominantly red tones a masked female nude, her long hair transforming her body into a version of the 1945 painting *The Rape*, mentioned earlier. She stands in a street, with a sheet-covered, ghost-like figure behind her and, beside her on the ledge against which she leans, the familiar Magrittean objects of a glass of water and a baguette. The transposition of face onto body (as Richard Calvocoressi points out in relation to *The Rape*[37]) introduces an element of the carnivalesque into the painting (as made explicit in the title *The Sage's Carnival*), connoting the bearded ladies and over-hirsute figures often found in circus sideshows, such as the hypertrichotic 'Lionel the Lion-faced Man' (Stephan Bibrowski, 1890–1932), who was featured in the July 1929 *Variétés* issue 'Galerie de Phénomènes' and who toured Belgium with the Barnum & Bailey circus in the early twentieth century.

Little attention has been given to the relationship between Bataille and Magritte – Magritte's sleek, seemingly hyperrealist style fits uncomfortably with the dirty, earth-bound and carnal elements of Bataille's base materialism, with its interests in vulgarity, sexual profanity, abjection, disgust and the uncivilized. A significant exception to this lack of attention was the 2011 exhibition 'René Magritte: The Pleasure Principle' at Tate Liverpool, where Magritte's rarely seen suite of six illustrations for *Madame Edwarda* was shown. The room in which they were hung was curtained away and

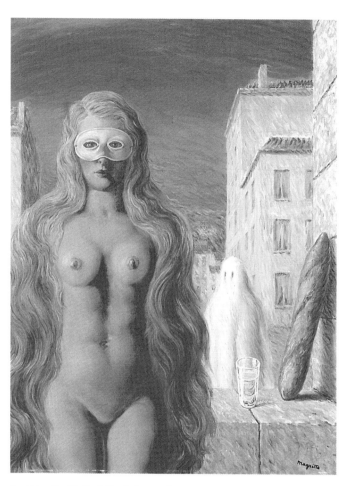

René Magritte, *The Sage's Carnival*, 1947, oil on canvas.

Postcard of Lionel the Lion-faced Man (Stephan Bibrowski, 1890–1932), *c.* 1910s.

accompanied by a parental warning, creating a secluded space apart from the rest of the exhibition, locating Magritte as peripheral to Bataillean thought just as criticism locates Bataille as peripheral to Magritte's oeuvre. Magritte's drawings are seen as a deviation (in every sense of the word) from his 'real' oeuvre, just as his art more generally 'deviates' intellectually and thematically from the concerns of Bretonian Surrealism's with realizing the potentials of the unconscious. The *Madame Edwarda* drawings represent another element of difference or differentiation within Magritte's work – another deviation from the critically accepted Magritte, just as, in the history of Surrealism, Bataille's thought constitutes a diversion from (or dangerous subversion of) the largely assimilated mainstream.

In the light of these internal differences within the oeuvre, the relation between Magritte and Bataille becomes potentially significant to an understanding of Magritte's work. Christoph Grunenberg identifies a range of associations between the two and suggests that

> Magritte would have felt an affinity with Bataille's provocative vision, himself employing at times in his art and writing

lewd sexual allusions and puns, vulgarity and profanity.
They also shared a fascination with crime as a means to
break through the facade of bourgeois normality.[38]

Grunenberg also identifies affinities between Bataille's notions of
l'informe, the formless, and Magritte's own destabilizing artistic
practices, including the 'Vache' period and what Grunenberg
calls its 'divergence from stylistic cohesion with the formal
integrity of objects, figures and patterns collapsing in painterly
expressiveness'.[39] While Magritte's 'sunlit' period introduces
carnivalesque elements, it is his 'Vache' period that allows for a
close mapping of Magritte's relations to the carnival and Bataille's
associated notions of excess. Despite his growing status as a
well-established artist in Belgium, the USA and Britain, his first
one-man exhibition in Paris came late in his career, eventually
being held from 11 May to 5 June 1948 in a minor dealer's gallery,
the Galerie du Faubourg. Magritte's pursuit of this exhibition
reveals the importance he set in being acknowledged by the French
avant-garde, and the level of disappointment and humiliation he
must have felt over the years at the repeated rebuffs by Breton and
the French art scene. It is therefore all the more interesting that,
far from settling back into his pre-1940s style, Magritte produced
specifically for this exhibition, over a period of five weeks, around
forty paintings and gouaches in a distinct new style which he
called 'Vache'. The term literally means 'cow', but also refers in
French to a lazy person or an exceptionally corpulent woman,
while amour vache (cow love) describes a relationship that is carnal
rather than affectionate – terms that indicate a certain coarseness
in these paintings and highlight their carnivalesque elements of
excess.

The colour palette of these pictures is loud and wild, ironically
referencing the work of the Fauves (wild beasts), a loose group of
early twentieth-century artists that included Henri Matisse and

André Derain, who typically used wild brushwork and distinctly vibrant colours. Magritte's *The Famine* (1948) epitomizes this style and draws on the Belgian artist James Ensor's *Skeletons Fighting over a Pickled Herring* from 1891. Mariën, commenting on this new style in the first issue of *Les lèvres nues*, wrote of Magritte 'improvising a series of grotesque and unbridled images, reflecting what might almost be called a desperate energy'.[40] Rather than impressing Parisian audiences, Magritte's aim was to give them 'an eyeful!'[41]

The exhibition was poorly received. A piece in *Arts* from 14 May 1948 reveals the reviewer's puzzlement: 'The present exhibition shows us a completely new Magritte . . . From the formal point of view . . . Magritte seems sometimes to have confused freedom and laxity.'[42] No works were sold, and Magritte was disappointed by Éluard's failure to support the exhibition by buying a piece. In a letter dated 17 May 1948 to Scutenaire and Irène Hamoir, he summarized the public and critical response:

> At the exhibition, there are visitors – (young girls have a tendency to laugh, but they control themselves because laughter is out of place in art galleries). Visitors who utter the usual bullshit. 'It's less profound than previously', it's 'Belgian wit', 'you can tell it's not Parisian'.[43]

Alexander Iolas, Magritte's post-war American dealer, made his dislike for the images clear in a letter of 21 November 1948:

> The people who like your pre-1940 painting do so unanimously because they find it more poetic and superior to those 5 [Impressionist] pictures I sent back to you and they are very keen to acquire the old ones . . . Nor do I ask you to copy the old pictures, but only not to break with the mysterious, poetic quality of your former pictures, which by their compact technique were much

more Magritte than those in which the Renoiresque
technique and colouring strike everyone as outmoded.[44]

Magritte returned to his 'signature' style soon after.

The 'Renoir' or 'sunlit' period, as critically neglected as the
'Vache' one, began in 1943 and thus coincided with Magritte signing
the tract against Bataille. It saw him turning to Impressionist
techniques executed with vibrant, sometimes even garish colour
schemes that emphasize illicit or erotic pleasure and evoke the
demotic shades of the carnival. These works drew heavily on
Renoir, and Magritte's aim was to represent a literal 'charm'
offensive against the menace of the Second World War. In May
1940 he had fled Belgium after the German invasion, temporarily
relocating first in Paris and then in Carcassonne with Scutenaire
and Hamoir before returning to Brussels in July. Georgette
remained in Brussels, partly because she was engaged in an affair
with the writer Paul Colinet. Magritte had visited London several
times during the late 1930s and, on one of these occasions, had
allegedly started an affair with the performance artist Sheila
Legge (1911–1949), who had famously paraded at the opening of
the International Surrealist Exhibition of 1936 as the 'Surrealist
Phantom', her head completely obscured by a bunch of flowers.
Georgette's liaison with Colinet seems to have been a vengeful
response to Magritte's infidelity.

His colourful, Renoiresque Impressionist style culminated in
Magritte's post-war tract *Le Surréalisme en plein soleil* (Surrealism
in Full Sunlight), published in October 1946, signed by Nougé,
Mariën, Scutenaire and other Belgians, which could be said to
constitute a third Surrealist manifesto. In a letter to Breton of 25
June 1946, Magritte proclaims a new age – the *période solaire*:

The painting of my 'solar period' is obviously in contradiction to many things we were convinced of before 1940 . . . The confusion and panic that Surrealism wanted to create in order to bring everything into question were achieved much better by the Nazi idiots than by us, and there was no question of avoiding the consequences . . . In opposition to the general pessimism, I set the search for joy, for pleasure. I feel it lies with us, who have some notion of how feelings are invented, to make joy and pleasure, which are so ordinary and beyond our reach, accessible to us all.[45]

Breton's response was extremely negative. In his text 'Devant le rideau' (In Front of the Curtain), written in 1947 for an exhibition catalogue, he opposed the attitude that artists should 'foster in their works only that which was "charm, pleasure, sunshine, objects of desire" and excluded anything that might be "sadness, boredom, threatening objects"!' He compared the position to a backward child insisting on fixing the needle of a barometer to 'fair' in order to ensure a day of sunshine.[46] Magritte considered the statement another 'excommunication' from Surrealism.

During this period Magritte's publications reveal many typically Bataillean interventions into religion and politics. This is evident, for example, in *The Three Tracts* – entitled *L'Imbécile, L'Emmerdeur* and *L'Enculeur* (Idiot, Silly Bugger and Fucker)[47] – published in 1946, the year of Magritte's *Madame Edwarda* illustrations. The tracts' contents evoke Bataillean thought and imagery with comments such as 'All the time, every day, at least one patriot has no qualms about shitting on the sacred soil of his native land' (*L'Imbécile*) and 'Really, when they take Christ's body into themselves they're swallowing the Lord's prick and arse too' (*L'Enculeur*).[48]

The illustrations for *Madame Edwarda* show that Magritte understood the content of Bataille's narrative and its philosophical and theoretical implications. The story concerns the narrator's increasing involvement in an erotic, pornographic and delirious relationship with the prostitute Madame Edwarda. Magritte's illustrations, reproducing the dreamlike atmosphere of the text, also closely relate to key passages. The winged penis alludes to the opening of the story where the narrator slips off his pants while wandering naked, sexually aroused and drunk, through the streets of Paris. The illustration of the masturbating priest recalls Madame Edwarda's words, hurled at the narrator: 'But you, you fake priest. I shit on you,'[49] while the illustration of the oversized phallus in a coach evokes Madame Edwarda's sexual encounter with a taxi driver on the back seat of his car.[50] The small, lonely, bowler-hatted man standing in front of the Courbet-like representation of a looming, oversized female crotch alludes to the following passage:

> She was seated, she held one leg stuck up in the air, to open her crack yet wider she used fingers to draw the folds of skin apart . . . 'You can see for yourself', she said, 'I'm GOD' . . . God figured as a public whore and gone crazy.[51]

Magritte's pictures elaborate Bataille's argument in *Eroticism* about the erotic 'opening directly out upon a certain vista of anguish, upon a certain lacerating consciousness of distress'.[52] But they are also poetic – as Bataille's description of his *Olympia* (1947), reproduced in *The Tears of Eros*, states: 'Eroticism cannot be entirely revealed without poetry.'[53] There is a clearly comical element to these illustrations, with their infantile obsession with genitalia and their disproportionate sizes. Feelings constantly shift between anguish and the absurd, the structures evoke children's book illustrations, and the cartoonish representations of objects such as the taxi and the winged penis set against a sunset further accentuate the comical tone.

The difference within repetition that organizes Magritte's work is demonstrated in these illustrations. Familiar Magritte motifs such as the fragmented female body and the bowler-hatted man encounter unfamiliar pornographic combinations of objects and environments. These juxtapositions produce further comic dimensions in the illustrations, heightening their violence and violation – a woman's mouth is sealed by a penis growing out of it, a female head is replaced by a penis transforming literally, in a rebus-like manner, into a *tête de nœud*, a dickhead. Laughter ruptures the viewer's environment, attenuating the wry humour more characteristically associated with Magritte's art, and causing what Bataille describes as a 'compenetration (contagion) [which] sets two worlds against each other and limits itself to a transition', a space where the viewer falls into the *other* world.[54] The role played by laughter as an invited response to Magritte's works (with their references to circus, cinema, and, as we will see, conjuring and other forms of comedic modernity) resembles that identified by Mikhail Bakhtin in his book on Rabelais and carnivalesque laughter, in which he argues (in terms that might well be describing a painting by Magritte) that

[laughter] has a deep philosophical meaning, it is one of the essential forms of the truth concerning the world as a whole, concerning history and man; it is a peculiar point of view relative to the world; the world is seen anew, no less (and perhaps more) profoundly than when seen from the serious standpoint.[55]

Magritte's illustrations for Bataille's book open a space for the subversive comic potentials of his art to find full expression. Far from being marginal to the main body of his work, they express its central concerns, confirming that Magritte's Surrealism is closer in spirit to Bataille's maverick project than the Bretonian variety with which he is usually compared and from which he was consistently ostracized. The six illustrations demonstrate most clearly that at the heart of the critically conventional readings of Magritte's oeuvre resides a repressed, critically disruptive inconsistency unassimilated into critical discourse, a comic expression of the multitude of carnivalesque, popular-cultural moments and experiences of fleeting pleasure, transient giddiness and magical transportation that deeply influenced Magritte from the earliest stages of his career.

6

Now You See Him,
Now You Don't . . .

In Chapter Four we considered the importance of the innovative technologies of the visual available in the modern fairground. Fairs also offered encounters with older forms of illusion to do with stage magic, prestidigitation, conjuring, deception and misdirection – trickery from which early cinematic forms clearly derived.[1] Critics have always constructed Magritte as a kind of magician – he was described by René Gaffé in the catalogue of the Exeter exhibition 'The Enchanted Domain' (1967) as 'the magician of unforeseen affinities', and in 2006 Marina Warner compared Magritte and Breton as intellectual magicians with contrasting styles: 'Whereas Breton is a conjuror who lets nothing slip, Magritte makes plain his sleights of hand, forcing us to see his riddles as riddles, and never taking pity and allowing a solution.'[2] This chapter will focus on the third major arena of the modern spectacle (after the circus and the cinema) to influence Magritte's art, that of stage magic, with all the optical trickery on which it relies and the iconographies of performance and deception through which the stage magician has been marketed in modernity.

Magic and illusionism flourished in Europe and America around the turn of the century, at a moment when new scientific discoveries and the development of filmic and photographic processes stirred popular imagination and both facilitated and necessitated (for competitive reasons) the rapid development of new magical methods. This flourishing also coincides again with

Magritte's childhood and youth. The popularity of magic shows in the late nineteenth century meant that many authors published widely read manuals for amateur magicians. These included Howard Thurston's *Card Tricks* (1903), Jean Eugène Robert-Houdin's *Confidences et révélations: Comment on deviant sorcier* (Confidences and Revelations: How One Can Become a Magician), first published in 1868 and frequently reprinted around the *fin de siècle*, and Louis Hoffmann's *Modern Magic* (1876). Funfairs of the Grande Fêtes Foraines typically included (as announced in an advert in *La Meuse* for a Liège funfair of 5 June 1909) 'Grand Theatre, Liege Puppet Theatre, Walloon Cabaret and a Magic Theatre'.[3] Magic shows were also part of circus performances. The Cirque des Variétés toured the country and showed, together with acrobatic dancers, musicians, singers, comedians, trapeze artists and other curiosity artists, 'le prestidigitateur mystérieux' (the mysterious conjuror).[4] Mystery, a vital element of the successful magician's performance, was of course a key facet of Magritte's oeuvre and of Surrealist art more broadly.

Many magicians, such as Chevalier Ernest Thorn or Horace Goldin, toured Belgium (the latter's revue was announced in *Le Soir* on 8 June 1913 as a 'kind of classical short course on what Bosco, Houdin, Herrmann the Great, Ching-Lin-Foo and other magicians have done').[5] *Prestidigitateurs* often featured in Belgian newspapers like *Le Soir* and *Journal de Charleroi*, gaining publicity by exposing the then popular mediumistic and spiritualistic practices as frauds – in 1906 the *Journal de Charleroi* reported on the famous London illusionist John Nevil Maskelyne's exposure of the American Davenport brothers' seances as 'trucs spirit' (spirit trickery),[6] and on M. Dicksonn's performative restaging (and thus debunking) of a seance.[7] This emerging brand of modern magic distanced itself from, and often sought to expose and debunk, the clairvoyant and spiritualist claims of the nineteenth century. A key strategy in the modern magician's exposure of spiritualism was the publication of books revealing the secrets behind magic tricks, some of which Magritte may have read, such as Pierre-Marie-André De Rocroy's *Trucs et secrets dévoilés par le mystérieux De Rocroy* (Tricks and Secrets Unveiled by the Mysterious De Rocroy; 1928), *Les Secrets de la Prestidigitation* (The Secrets of Conjuring) by St J. de l'Escap (1907), or *Houdini's Paper Magic* (1922) by Harry Houdini.

The pervasive presence of magic and magicians within popular culture and the everyday environs of bourgeois life during Magritte's youth and early career was indicated by the proliferation of advertising posters exploiting new stone lithographic and letterpress printing techniques and innovations of colour reproduction.[8] These posters would have captured the young Magritte's attention, and they later influenced his own commercial poster design work. The connection is clear between professional magicians' debunking of fraudulent spiritualist or mediumistic applications of their craft and Magritte's insistent intellectual inquiries into, and revelations of, the illusions underlying the deceptions of the image, the primary mode of marketing in the twentieth century.

Prestidigitation was also a major popular amusement during Magritte's time in Paris from September 1927. A *Paris-soir* article of 18 June 1927 headed 'Le parfait prestidigitateur' (The Perfect Conjuror) elaborates that 'We now have in France . . . three thousand conjurors,' a demography that influenced in subtle ways the development of French Surrealism and related avant-gardes.[9] Van Hecke's multidisciplinary journal *Variétés*, to which Magritte was a frequent contributor, clearly alludes in its title to variety shows in circuses and theatres, and its contents point to the interest of the Brussels Surrealist group in the popular spaces of the circus, music hall and magic shows. While the circus was a recurrent reference point – the very first issue, of 15 May 1929, carried advertisements for Marcel Vertès' *Le Cirque* works, and the 15 April 1930 issue juxtaposed a group portrait of Van Hecke, Albert

Valentin, Denis Marion and Mesens with other photographs of the Fratellini brothers, Chaplin and the clown Dario. The 15 October 1929 issue of *Variétés* focused largely on the field of magic, from occult magic to stage conjuring.

Early cinema shared close connections with the long-established traditions of illusionism and stage magic. Projection technologies enabled magic tricks and fake seances, and early cinematographers such as Émile and Vincent Isola and Georges Méliès were originally stage magicians. Méliès (1861–1938) attended magic show performances at London's Egyptian Hall (run by Maskelyne) and Paris's Theatre Robert-Houdin (founded by the magician Jean Eugène Robert-Houdin), and later even purchased the theatre. Méliès added cinema to his theatrical repertoire and directed over five hundred films, many of which drew on magic tricks – as Lynda Nead observes, he used 'the full range of magic theatre and film trickery to create a visual conversation between the pictorial arts', just as Magritte would in his paintings.[10] Méliès' silent short film *The House of Mystery* (1901), for example, displays a vast treasure box of magic tricks, from skeleton-to-human transformation – as imitated by Magritte in his 1935 painting of a skull-headed female nude in *The Bungler* (see p. 197) – to levitation.

Magritte would certainly have seen many of Méliès' films, as their popularity ensured them frequent screenings across Europe and America in fairgrounds and music halls as well as in cinemas. Méliès himself toured Europe, including Brussels, in 1910, and his films were often rescreened in Belgium during the war, as discussed earlier. After a brief waning of public interest in his work (cinema audiences being notoriously fickle and subject to the influence of shifts in technology, such as the development of talking pictures in 1927, rendering older, silent movies slightly passé), he was rediscovered by several journalists, generating new interest in France at the time that Magritte was resident in Paris. The revival culminated in a special issue of *La Revue du cinéma* (15 October 1929) and a gala retrospective of Méliès' work in December 1929 at the Salle Pleyel.

In Magritte's *The Silence of Smiling* (1928) four near-identical grinning male heads are suspended against a dark background.[11] This painting was produced around the time of the rediscovery of Méliès' work in France. The four suspended heads seem to refer to Méliès' filming of a magic trick in *The Four Troublesome Heads* (1898). Featuring one of the first known uses of the special effect of multiple exposure of objects on a black background, it shows Méliès as a magician standing between two tables. The trick sees him magically removing one head from his shoulders, followed by another which manifests itself while he places the first head on the table. The film concludes with three identical disembodied heads laid on a table, with a fourth on Méliès' shoulders, leaving *Four Troublesome Heads*. Magritte may well have thought of this film and its English title when painting *The Silence of Smiling*.

The painting's focus is on the faces, their seriality and their floating in darkness. These techniques recall strategies used

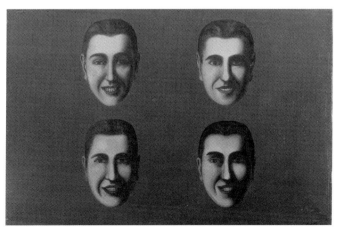

René Magritte, *The Silence of Smiling*, 1928, oil on canvas.

From George Méliès' *Un homme de têtes* (The Four Troublesome Heads; 1898).

in silent movies to represent (unheard) speakers and to convey emotions, as well as (following cartoon conventions) to show multiple or conflicting identities residing within a single person. These techniques are used, for example, in the opening scenes of Fritz Lang's *Doctor Mabuse the Gambler* (1922), where the doctor's disguise is shown in different photographs of his face, and soon after a close-up is provided of him speaking. In Robert Wiene's *The Cabinet of Dr Caligari* (1920) the camera focuses on the somnambulist Cesare's intense face, his kohl-lined eyes seeming to float in the air; and in *Fantômas in the Shadow of the Guillotine* (1913), René Navarre, as Fantômas, stares directly into the camera as his visage changes into several disguises he uses during the film.

The staple tricks of magic acts take everyday objects out of their familiar contexts and perform impossible feats with them – making things and people appear or disappear, changing the sizes of things, or apparently defeating gravity by levitation. Magritte employed similar effects in many of his paintings, notably calling them 'la mise en scène d'objets' (the staging of objects) in his 'systematic search for a disturbing poetic effect'.[12] A painterly imitation of levitation is apparent, for example, in *Archimedes' Principle* (which exists in two versions dated 1950 and 1952), in which apples float, in defiance of the gravity they confirmed for Newton. In 'Lifeline 1' Magritte comments on his use of such devices as

> the creation of new objects; the transformation of familiar objects; changing the constitution of certain objects: a sky made of wood, for example; the use of words with images; calling an image by the wrong name; putting into practice ideas suggested by friends; portraying certain visions of the half-awake state were, on the whole, ways to force objects to be sensational at last . . . I was blamed for lots of . . . things and finally for showing objects in pictures in unfamiliar places. And yet, here, it is a question of making a real if unconscious desire come true. Indeed, the ordinary painter is already trying, with the limits fixed for him, to upset the order in which he always sees objects.[13]

Many of Magritte's works refer directly to stage magic, such as *The Magic Light* (1928), *The Magic Mirror* (1929), *The Magician's Accomplices* (1926, see p. 207) and *Daily Magic* (1952). The titles exploit the connotations of the French word *magie* (magic) and its echo of the words 'image' and 'imagination' (not to mention its repetition of the first three letters of the name Magritte). In other instances, Magritte's titles have the rhetorical structure (usually along the lines of 'The + adjective + noun' or 'The + noun + possessive'), style and poetic resonances of names of magic illusions advertised on posters and adverts for magic shows. A poster for M. Evanion (the stage name of Harry Evans) announces tricks such as the Sympathetic Maps, the Fabulous Egg, the Magic Candle, the Birth of Flowers and the Enchanted Flag – titles that echo in, or are partly and sometimes fully repeated by, Magritte's own titles, such as *La Vie secrète* (The Secret Life; 1928), *Le Drapeau noir* (The Black Flag; 1937), *Le Miroir vivant* (The Living Mirror; 1928), *La Naissance des fleurs* (The Birth of Flowers; 1929) and *Le Soupçon mystérieux* (The Mysterious Suspicion; 1927).

Magritte's conceptual preoccupations can often be understood in terms of magical performances. Questions of 'appearance' are a recurrent concern: in a letter to the French Cartesian philosopher Ferdinand Alquié on 11 June 1959, Magritte comments:

> I think (as well as possible) about this question of 'appearance' and of that which it may hide. I do not succeed in believing that there is something underneath appearance other than appearance, and under this, into infinity, always appearance.[14]

Critics often interpret Magritte's works as inquiries into the relations between reality and representation; reading them from a stage magician's perspective gives them new resonances. Magritte wrote to Duchamp in 1966 using the discourse of the magician in order to explain his work:

> You rightly say that the possible derives from the impossible. And indeed, the *visible* description (a painted picture) of an *invisible* thought (which consists of visible figures arranged in a certain order), is something 'possible impossible' or, in other words, something 'visible invisible'.[15]

The *Conjuror's Repository*, a late eighteenth-century compendium of tricks, lists 'Visible Invisible', an old feat in which writing appears and disappears on a mirror, as if by magic.[16]

Magritte's long-term deployment of the rhetoric of magic as a discursive tool to elaborate his concepts is also evidenced in an essay titled 'Leçon de choses' (Object Lessons) published in 1962 in the journal *Rhétorique*. In it he elaborates on the potential for ambiguity in the relationship between image and connotation. In each of the examples he cites, the image depicts one set of possible meanings while the caption opens and explores the space between these possibilities. The first two examples exploit elements of the visual rhetoric of the magician – one shows three sketches of a magician taking off his hat, then taking off his whole head (recalling, once again, Méliès' *Four Troublesome Heads*), before replacing the hatted head upside down; and the second reproduces Magritte's *The Magician* (see p. 182) to emphasize how perception can be deceived, or diverted, tricked or simply refused.[17]

Christopher Priest, in his novel *The Prestige* (1995), provides a useful taxonomy of the magic act (and adds a new term, the 'prestige', to the vocabulary of magic):

> An illusion has three stages.
>
> First there is the setup, in which the nature of what might be attempted at is hinted at, or suggested, or explained. The apparatus is seen. Volunteers from the audience sometimes participate in preparation. As the trick is being set up, the magician will make every possible use of misdirection.
>
> The performance is where the magician's lifetime of practice, and his innate skill as a performer, conjoin to produce the magical display.
>
> The third stage is sometimes called the effect, or the prestige, and this is the product of magic. If a rabbit is pulled from a hat, the rabbit, which apparently did not exist before the trick was performed, can be said to be the prestige of that trick.[18]

A similar sequence operates in Magritte's work. If concepts of mystery, appearance and disappearance are traits shared by magicians and Magritte, so is the repertoire of objects they employ – hats (from the well-known bowler to top hats like that depicted in *The Handsome Brooder* (1950), where a face emerges from the hat's material), doves, umbrellas, roses, daggers, apples, keys, eggs, candles, mirrors, cages, frames, boxes, cases and suitcases, tables presenting objects, windows, glasses of water and screens are all items of equipment used by both in their performances. They are also staple objects in early twentieth-century books on magic tricks. Arthur Good (under the pseudonym Tom Tit) and Louis Poyet's three-volume collaboration *La Science amusante* (1890–93) collects material originally featured in the magazine *L'Illusion*. These volumes were often reprinted during the twentieth century, and extracts from them were reproduced in various publications, such as *The Boy's Own Paper* or *Beeton's Boy's Own Magazine*.

La Science amusante 'popularised the marvels of science',[19] presenting scientific experiments as magic tricks using everyday objects in domestic settings – an iconography familiar from Magritte's own magical scenes. An abridged anthology in English, titled *100 Amazing Magic Tricks* and translated from the 1891 edition originally published by Larousse, includes the trick 'The Magic Box', which shows a child peering through a peephole on the other side of which a box is shown operated by two hands. The trick is accompanied by the teaser question, 'How would you like to change one object into a totally different one before the eyes of your audience? Make up this magic box and you will be able to do just that.'[20] The large printed heading of the trick 'No Need for a Mirror to Reflect Life' announces that 'Some of the most baffling tricks invented by famous magicians are based on optical illusions . . . Using mirrors, magicians can make things seem to appear and disappear.'[21] Magritte's mirrors perform similar magical reflections, offering impossible views. In *The Magic Mirror* (1929) we expect to see a reflection of a human being in a mirror facing the viewer, but find instead the words 'corps humain' (human body) – a version of the fairy tale mirror that, infallibly honest, offers only intimations of the inevitable mortality of those who gaze into it (a premonition, perhaps, of the 'mirror stage' theorized in 1936 by the psychoanalyst Jacques Lacan, in which the human infant misrecognizes its mirror image as itself).[22] In *Not to Be Reproduced* (1937) a 'reversed' portrait of the British Surrealist and collector Edward James (1907–1984) faces a mirror reflecting not the face we (viewing him from behind) cannot see, but instead a repetition of the back of the man's head – the mirror displays what we can already see. The only thing accurately reflected here (that is, reversed in the mirror) is a book with inscriptions on its cover, a copy of Charles Baudelaire's 1857 translation of Edgar Allan Poe's 1838 novel *The Narrative of Arthur Gordon Pym of Nantucket* (Magritte owned this and many other works by Poe, one of his favourite authors). This image, its moody mirror also evoking the looking glass in *Alice's Adventures in Wonderland*, is a *portrait manqué* (failed portrait) – a term Paul Colinet used to describe a 'new potential in Magritte's images that had been constantly recurring in his work of a decade: the back view, the missing face, the mirror'.[23]

As is the case with all magicians, containers are important in Magritte's practice. Examples range from boxes and other encasements in his images to bottles on which he painted. These elements present us with a series of magical stage set-ups, preparing the viewer for a performance of aesthetic prestidigitation. On these stages – reminiscent of the stage of the magic performance, its wooden floor and velvet curtains connoting in turn the magic theatres of the nineteenth century – Magritte uses the props of the magicians and their techniques to perform the painterly illusion of making ordinary objects extraordinary.

Conjuring Biography

Once we have the technique, the props and the stage, we of course also need, most importantly, the magician himself. Magritte's self-constructions in various autobiographical fragments emphasize the magical at key moments and as key characteristics in his portrayal of himself. As noted earlier, the lecture 'Lifeline I' was delivered at Antwerp's Musée Royal des Beaux-Arts in November 1938, and published in the Belgian journal *Combat* on 10 December. Magritte and Scutenaire produced a second, rewritten version ('Lifeline II') for inclusion in the appropriately titled Belgian publication *L'Invention collective* (April 1940). These differing versions of an ostensibly straightforward autobiographical narrative immediately call into question narrative reliability – which version is the most authentic or accurate autobiography? Which is the 'true' narrative, the 'real' version of the narrating self?

The contents of these two versions of 'Lifeline' also point to the narrative's unreliability. Magritte's autobiographical account of his development as an artist begins with painting itself as a magical act in his encounter with a painter, identified as Léon Huygens,[24] probably in 1911 or 1912 in the old cemetery in Soignies, disused after 1890. Magritte's encounter probably occurred during one of his regular summer holidays in Soignies with his paternal grandmother Marie, his aunts Flora and Maria (his godmother) and the latter's husband, Firmin Desaunois (whose long moustache Magritte admired). Magritte tells the story in 'Lifeline I':

> In my childhood, I used to enjoy playing with a little girl in the old disused cemetery in a small provincial town. We visited the underground vaults, whose heavy iron door we could lift up, and we would come up into the light, where a painter from the capital was painting in a very picturesque avenue in the cemetery with its broken stone pillars strewn with dead leaves. The art

of painting then seemed to me to be vaguely magical [*vaguement magique*], and the painter gifted with superior powers.[25]

The rewritten version of this passage in 'Lifeline II' further emphasizes this magic: 'When I came up into the light, I discovered one day in midst of broken stone pillars strewn over by dead leaves, a painter who came from the capital who seemed to perform a magical act [*une action magique*].'[26]

The rough manuscript for a lecture Magritte delivered in London in 1937, preceding his first solo show in Britain at the London Gallery in April 1938, again describes (in terms echoing 'Lifeline I') the revelatory moment of encountering the painter in the cemetery: 'At the time the art of painting seemed to me to be vaguely magical, and the painter to be endowed with superior powers.'[27] The magical, mentioned in all these accounts, is a significant enough element to retain in each rewrite. The meaning is consistent: art reveals itself to Magritte in a moment of magical experience, becoming a 'reference point' to return to within his autobiography (perhaps not unlike the theatrical stages and places of his childhood explored above). As he remarks, 'I had a reference point which placed me elsewhere: that magical art that I had known in my childhood.'[28]

Magical imagery and connotations are also fundamental to another formative moment in Magritte's life, as he narrates in the first version of 'Lifeline':

One night in 1936, I awoke in a room in which [some]one has placed a cage with a bird, which has fallen asleep. A magnificent error allowed me to see, in the cage, the vanished bird, and an egg which had replaced it.[29]

For Magritte, the bird–egg revelation became the beginning of his 'research, which was an attempt to solve a problem'.[30] Magritte's narrative plays out in two paintings – *Elective Affinities*, painted

René Magritte, *Elective Affinities*, 1933, oil on canvas.

in 1933 before his apparent epiphany of 1936 (highlighting the unreliability of his autobiographical narrative) and *Clairvoyance* (1936), a self-portrait of the artist in the act of painting a bird on a canvas while observing an egg. The painted bird is a version of an earlier painting from 1935, as well as a one-to-one adaptation of a *Larousse* illustration of a nightingale in a chart of 'useful birds'.[31]

Eggs are, of course, part of a magician's repertoire (a poster from about 1910 shows 'Thurston the Great Magician' framed by red curtains, adding another magically produced egg to an oversized pile from which others are tumbling, while the poster announces 'Eggs Extraordinary'). Magritte also alludes to 'Columbus's Trick – The Standing Egg' when he depicts an egg-shaped rock balancing atop a cliff in *The Glass Key* (1959). The illusion is explained in Pinetti's *Repository*:

> To make an egg stand on end on any polished surface seems very extraordinary, yet it is to be done, even on a *looking-glass*; now from the form of an *egg* nothing is more liable to roll, and on nothing more so than a looking-glass; to accomplish this trick, let the performer take an egg in his hand, and while he keeps talking, and staring in the face of his audience, give it two or three hearty shakes, which will break the yolk, which will sink to one end, and consequently make it more heavy.[32]

René Magritte, *Clairvoyance*, 1936, oil on canvas.

Poster for The Great Nesbitt Mysteries magic show (illustrating the 'The Giant's Breakfast' trick), *c.* 1920.

The turning of an egg into a bird, and vice versa, is an established magic trick that comes in many variations, such as the 'hatched bird' trick, where, as described in *The Boy's Own Conjuring Book* (1857), a live canary is hidden in a hollowed egg and then revealed. Such tricks were also staple cinema illusions: a scene from early in Muller's film *There It Is* (discussed earlier) uses jump cuts to show full-grown chickens hatching impossibly from eggs. The popularity of similar bird–egg illusion tricks can also be traced in a poster promoting 'The Great Nesbitt Mysteries: The Giant's Breakfast' from about 1920. Based on a David Devant illusion, the black shadow of the magician in this poster points to a giant egg sitting in a cage-like structure. The eggshell is broken on top and a full-grown bird peeps out at the viewer, while above it we see a shattered picture or mirror frame from which shards of glass have fallen (another recurrent motif of Magritte's, evident in works like *Evening Falls*, discussed below). Magritte's *Elective Affinities*, with its giant egg in a case, is remarkably similar to this representation of a magic trick, while the magician–egg–bird arrangement recalls that of *Clairvoyance*, in which Magritte constructs himself as a prestidigitator. Even the title, *Clairvoyance*, and the depiction of the painter's sleight of hand, evoke the prestidigitator's debunking of clairvoyant and other spiritualist activities mentioned above. In *The Healer* of 1937, his self-portrait-as-conjuror, he replaces the body of a sitting male figure with a birdcage containing doves, sitting beside a mysterious bag (of tricks?). Over the birds is draped a red theatrical curtain, recalling magic acts in which birds and cages disappear. In a different version of this picture, a gouache on paper from 1946, the link to magic is clearer still. Here, hat and red drape frame the seated man's body, which consists of a sheet of paper including, as in a magician's act, four symbolic objects – pipe, key, glass and dove – while a suitcase is positioned on the man's left.

Magritte represents himself as prestidigitator in *The Magician* of 1951, a painting in which the influence of cinematic imagery

René Magritte, *The Magician*, 1951, oil on canvas.

and techniques clearly overlaps with that of stage magic (and
indicating the degree of equivalence that existed between the
two in Magritte's deployment of them). The painting shows
Magritte taking a meal. Formally dressed, his arms and hands
have multiplied to show in a single image various movements of
eating and drinking simultaneously, emphasizing in a comic way
the magician's ambidexterity. The painting condenses the frame-
by-frame cinematic images of narrative sequentiality, a Muybridge
study of movement in reverse, transforming an image of motion
into one of stillness. Magritte assembles the segments of sliced-up
movement into one image to create a slightly disturbing effect of
dynamic stasis. In his 'Object Lessons' article of 1962 Magritte
remarked on his use of movement images to produce static ones:
'Neither those obsessed with movement nor those obsessed with
immobility, will find this image to their taste.'[33] This preoccupation
with the differences between the otherwise comparable magics of

Poster advertising the magician Roody, 1930.

cinema and painting is evident in many of Magritte's remarks. For example, in Jacques de Decker's 1960 interview with him, which focuses on cinema, Magritte discusses a 1959 film of himself: 'I'm of the opinion that Luc de Heusch's film has not exposed me . . . Film is the art of movement, and the representations of my pictures, which one can see on my canvases, are in their existence static.'[34]

Magritte's remark also suggests a magician's concern with protecting the workings of his own tricks from being revealed to the public. The depiction of his own painterly 'sleight of hand' – an allegory of his creativity as an artist – is remarkably similar to a poster advertising a performance from the late 1920s of the Italian-born illusionist Roody. Known for his sleight-of-hand tricks, Roody performed across Europe. The poster shows a simulated time-lapse effect of Roody's hand movement, emphasizing his skill with prestidigitation techniques. We see the magician in profile, looking at his hand, in a composition not dissimilar to Magritte's *The Mysterious Suspicion*, the 1928 painting referenced the following year in *Un Chien andalou*. A 1926 article in *Paris-soir* identifies the 'principal qualities of a conjuror':

> First of all a supreme manual skill. Then a thorough knowledge of all sciences: physics, chemistry, electricity, mathematics, psychology. Finally, and most importantly, a great presence of mind: this is how you should never miss a turn.[35]

The polymathic knowledge required of the successful conjuror also encompassed art, staging and the performance of comedy, crime and tragedy, and cut across science and mysticism. Surrealism, too, was polymathic in its intellectual range. The 'cabinets of curiosities' assembled by Surrealist collectors like Breton and the English artist and collector Roland Penrose (1900– 1984) offer evidence of a remarkable range of academic inquiry, as do the Surrealist *dérives* (drifts) through the Paris flea markets at

Clignancourt, mapping and excavating the secret histories of the city and the discarded objects that gave it texture. Publications such as Georges Bataille's *Documents* actively explored the unexpected relations between diverse, distinct and distant cultural realities. The magician's polymathic agility and depth, giving him the ability to deceive even the most attentive of audiences, make him a prime figure for the pursuit and representation of such knowledge, and from it the creation of new marvellous realities.

7

Disappearing Acts

A number of Magritte's old friendships in France and Belgium became rather fragile from the mid-1950s, in the last decade of his life, and key contemporaries were disappearing. The French poet Paul Éluard, with whom Magritte had exchanged portraits in the mid-1930s, died in 1952.[1] Yves Tanguy died in 1955, and Camille Goemans in 1960. Paul Nougé's behaviour became increasingly difficult – around 1951 he was dismissed from the Laboratoire de Biologie Chimique, where he had worked since 1919, for heavy drinking, and Magritte and Georgette broke off contact with him. Without a job or a pension, Nougé was forced to sell his small collection of Magritte works. Meanwhile, Magritte's relations with the French Surrealists continued to be strained. In 1954, 24 works by Magritte were included in the Belgian pavilion of the Venice Biennale, which took Surrealism as its main theme. While Magritte was very popular at the biennale, there was a growing discontent among Breton's followers with the older generation of figurative Surrealist painters, including Magritte. Max Ernst, for example, was denounced and excommunicated for accepting the festival's major painting prize, and Mesens warned Magritte that his works were being boycotted.[2] These rumours of Parisian discontent, alongside a Breton-led drive to return to automatism, culminated in a misunderstanding by the Swiss artist Meret Oppenheim, who declared Magritte on the verge of suicide.[3]

Paul Colinet, whose affair with Georgette had been partially to blame for Magritte's temporary wartime relocation to France, died on 23 December 1957. The next day the Magrittes moved for the last time, into a detached house with garden – which Magritte regarded as 'tranquil' – at 97 rue des Mimosas in the Schaerbeek district of Brussels. George Melly described the house as

> a solid villa, the kind of property favoured by a well-established dentist. Inside everything was neat and highly polished, the furniture was comfortable but banal. In the living room, overlooking a well-kept garden, there was a small grand piano, draped silk curtains, manufactured 'oriental' rugs and two suspended gilt cherubs while, on every surface, were a collection of china birds and many novelty clocks which, more or less on the hour, struck and chimed.[4]

Magritte characteristically painted not in a studio but in a small room on the first floor, using an easel standing on an unprotected carpet. Betty Magritte, Paul Magritte's wife and collaborator, noted that he

> always preferred the kitchen table as his work place. Even in the rue des Mimosas, I have often seen him making drawings and sketches on the kitchen table! There, too, it was the lightest room in the house, because it got the sun most of the day.[5]

Through such social and artistic difficulties, Magritte sustained his lifelong identification with Fantômas, a figure closely connected to the assumed persona of the artist-magician. 'I *know* that I'm not Fantômas, but when my mind thinks Fantômas, it *is* Fantômas,' he told Jacques Goossens in 1966.[6] This connection, he thought, provided an overarching metaphor 'explaining' his own practice and his reluctance to theorize it. As late as 1957 (and despite their earlier disputes), Magritte responded to a five-question survey in the journal *Formes de l'art*, compiled by André Breton, on 'magical art', emphasizing his own comprehension of magic as a means of transcending the need for the mechanics of analysis: 'An object manifests a magical power when it enchants us without the intermediary of a methodical analysis . . . A magical conception of the world makes language *speak*, it does not analyse it.'[7] Such statements indicate how, late in his career, Magritte was prepared to use Surrealist conceptions of the magical to negate the need for rational inquiry into the effects of the work of art, and to connect his own work closely to the prestidigitator's elisions in the performance of trickery. Deceiving his victims through appearances (as a magician does), Fantômas is chased by the detective Juve; but he always escapes just as Juve thinks he is caught, a disappearance corresponding to the moment in the magic act ('the prestige') when the audience thinks it is witnessing the secret of the trick, but the secret escapes them.

Magritte's self-reflexive use of the magician's iconography is evident in a 1938 photograph of himself with his 1927 Fantômas painting *The Barbarian*. This photograph was taken at his first one-man show in London. It is the only record of the painting, which, together with others by Magritte, was destroyed during the first bombing raid on London. Like *The Flame Rekindled* the painting draws on the famous image of Fantômas in a top hat from the cover illustration of Allain and Souvestre's first 1911 novel. *The Barbarian* shows only Fantômas's face, staring back at the viewer. He is wearing a top hat and suit and seems to dissolve into the brick wall behind him. In the photograph, a bowler-hatted Magritte mimes the posture of Fantômas. Both wear the formal clothing, particularly the top hat, of the magician, the style conventions introduced by Robert-Houdin. The photograph displays several stage-magical connotations. Magritte clearly identifies with the character in the painting, transforming the photograph into a kind of double-self portrait. The painting shows Fantômas staring back at us, effectively performing (as he repeatedly does in the narratives) a disappearing act in plain view. Magritte, in contrast, constructs himself as magician, both authoring the magic act of the painting (as Allain and Souvestre do in their narratives) and, in imitating Fantômas, performing it. He both appears and disappears in this image, the artist becoming part of his artistic work, of his magic act.

The key element here is that of disappearance, which I want to read in this final chapter as a recurrent trope in Magritte's art, a metaphorical and prefigurative staging of the other 'disappearance' facing Magritte late in his life – that of death. The figure of Fantômas affords an extended performance of the artist's own mortality, mapped out in a career-long variety of Gothic tropes and tricks, all occurring within characteristically Magrittean images and iconographies. This final chapter traces some of the ways Magritte's art provided opportunities to stage performances of his own final disappearance.

The magician's skill in Magritte's paintings is located in its evident staging, in the deception of the viewer in plain sight. This applies to individual images and also to the oeuvre as a whole, in which prestidigitation is apparent everywhere. The thin white dotted line in *The Human Condition* is a clue for the viewer – a mark of the artifice of the work, its presence asserts that a trick is played (again, in plain sight), yet (such is the habit of looking for meaning, of seeking the solution to the question posed by the picture) the viewer still searches for what is behind the canvas (and is encouraged to do so by Magritte's own misdirecting comments). The pleasure produced by this game is precisely the pleasure Magritte evokes in us with many of his canvases – our vision is drawn along the dotted line of the painted canvas in *The Human Condition*, a hinge between 'I know well' (that this is a painting and not part of the landscape) and the 'but nonetheless' (the painting looks like the landscape), to a third dimension. The hinge between is just a preamble, a magician's misdirection (we are led to believe

that we are finding a 'solution' to how the trick is done while
the actual trick happens elsewhere) – there is no divide between
representation and reality, as all of this is 'just' a painting.

Magritte knows this, explaining in a comment which itself
could come from an instruction book for magic tricks: 'Everything
we see hides another thing; we always wish to see what is hidden
by what we see.'[8] What vanishes is what we want to see, and it
is concealed by that we wish to see beyond. A similar kind of
misdirection is also at work in the critical positioning of Magritte
(encouraged by his own sometimes cryptic commentary) as a
postmodernist/poststructuralist painter *avant la lettre*. The real
'trick' in Magritte's oeuvre, we might say, is the importance of
painterly prestidigitation – of pictorial trickery – as a significant,
theoretically supported procedure. His work becomes an extended
application of these tricks, a lifelong magic act in which Magritte-
the-performer repeatedly disappears, a vanishing performed in full
view and yet consistently able to deceive the viewer into attempting
to look beyond what is on display. This performance has the
added value of shifting Magritte-the-artist closer to Magritte-the-
entertainer, cementing his explicit rejection of bourgeois culture in
a repositioning of the status of the artist and his works. Again there
is a parallel with *Fantômas*, for as Matthieu Letourneux points out,
Allain and Souvestre's narratives are themselves heavily steeped in
stage magic and consciously participate 'in a popular culture far
away from any legitimate field of culture'.[9]

Magical Transformations

Magritte's relationship with the ever-vanishing Fantômas works
as a conduit for other aspects of his magician persona, enabling
us to link specific works to the iconography of stage magic as
well as to Gothic tropes connected with mortality, as seen in

advertising and promotional material on the walls of Paris and
Belgium during the 1920s. A poster from about 1922–4 shows
the music-hall illusionist Harry Cameron (1881–1944), known as
'Carmo', who toured Paris and Brussels in the 1920s and '30s and
was particularly famous for disappearing acts, including making
lions disappear and then reappear, as reported in the 18 June 1927
Paris-soir article mentioned earlier.[10] In the poster, his body seems
to fade, revealing the brick wall behind him – much as Fantômas
fades in *The Barbarian*. This illusion, 'Pepper's Ghost Effect',
named after its creator John Henry Pepper (1821–1900),[11] was often
performed in theatres, amusement parks, carnival sideshows and
fairs (including perhaps the one at which Magritte met Georgette).
This specific image of 'Pepper's Ghost Effect' may have inspired
Magritte's 1943 painting *Universal Gravitation*, in which the arm
of a hunter (based on a photograph of Louis Scutenaire) vanishes
into a brick wall.

One element of the 'Pepper's Ghost Effect' trick involves the
appearance on the magician or clairvoyant's command of ghostly
objects and people fading in or out of the room, or transforming
into different things. These are of course recurring themes in
Magritte's work from 1927 onwards, on which he comments in a
letter to Nougé in November 1927:

I think I have made a really striking discovery in painting. Up
to now I have used composite objects, or else the placing of
an object was sometimes enough to make it mysterious. But
as a result of the experiments I've made here, I have found a
new potential in things – their ability to become gradually
something else, an object merging into an object other than
itself. For instance the sky in certain places allows wood to show
through . . . By this means I produce pictures in which the eye
must 'think' in a completely different way from the usual one:
things are tangible and yet a few planks of solid wood become

imperceptibly transparent in certain places, or else a naked
woman has parts which also change into a different substance.[12]

Understanding the influences on Magritte of different traditions
outside those of art history, and recognizing the dynamic potentials
inherent in the cross-fertilization of popular cultures and
intermedial mixings of early modernism, enables us to recognize
these fades and transformations as painterly effects that combine
the illusionism of stage magic with the technical innovations of
cinematic fades. Another riff on 'Pepper's Ghost Effect', the self-
portrait *Attempting the Impossible* (1928), depicts the artist seemingly
painting his partner Georgette into life. Both are standing upright
in a room, and his eyes are concentrated on an incomplete painterly
detail of the the figure's arm. In this painting Magritte plays
Pygmalion to Georgette's Galatea.[13]

The pygmalionesque awakening-to-life of a representation
was another popular magic trick of the time, invented by David
Devant (often referred to as 'the greatest magician of all time').
First performed in 1893, the illusion was known as 'The Artist's
Dream'. The mechanism involved was devised and constructed
by Maskelyne and initially performed at Maskelyne & Cooke's
Egyptian Hall. In this illusion, a painting of the magician's
apparently dead accomplice is brought back to life, as if dreamed
into reality by her partner. A related trick, called 'spirit painting' or
tableau animé, was also popular around the same time, performed
by magicians such as Professor Herrmann (around 1900) and
depicted in posters by showing a living woman emerging from
a painted frame – a magical setting also staged in a photograph
taken in 1928 of Magritte in front of *Attempting the Impossible*. In
another poster from around 1894 promoting 'Maskelyne & Cooke's
Mysteries: The Artist's Dream', the artist sits asleep next to his work
while two ghostly, semi-transparent figures appear in the painting,
one lifting a heavy red curtain from the picture frame (objects

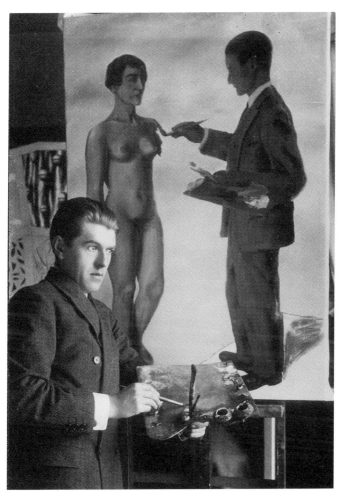
Photograph of Magritte painting *Attempting the Impossible*, 1928.

familiar from Magritte's paintings) to reveal the other stepping out of the frame – an animation we can also witness in Magritte's *The Light of Coincidences* (1933), where a ghostly torso seems to leave its picture frame.

A trick presenting the animation of a statue, which yet remains forbidden to the touch, was performed by the magician in Georges Méliès' film *The Magician* (1898), and Percy Stow's *An Animated Picture Studio* (also referred to as *An Up-to-date Studio*) of 1903 similarly plays with the pygmalionesque device of pictures coming to life. Its synopsis reads:

> A young dancer enters a photographic studio, is filmed dancing and sits on the photographer's knee. The resulting film is projected on to a picture frame. She protests and throws the frame to the floor, shattering it, but it continues to move.[14]

Poster for the show 'The Artist's Dream' by Maskelyne & Cooke, *c*. 1894.

René Magritte, *The Light of Coincidences*, 1933, oil on canvas.

The shattered image on the floor (reminiscent of the poster for 'The Giant's Breakfast' noted earlier), still moving and reproducing what was on the wall, recalls Magritte's painting *Evening Falls* (1964), in which a view out of a red-curtain-framed window on to a landscape is depicted. However, inside the room are shattered pieces of glass underneath the window, each shard a fragment of the exterior landscape, the fall of evening literalized as a falling of window and image.

The 'Pepper's Ghost Effect' trick was also extensively used in conjuring acts and seances to create the highly lucrative illusion of bringing the dead back to life. Cupboards, cabinets and coffins are key props in these versions of the trick. A poster of around 1891 promoting Harry Kellar's famous Spirit Cabinet announces 'Kellar and his Perplexing Cabinet Mysteries'. We can trace the influence of cabinets in stage magic (exploited to powerful Gothic effect by

Wiene in *The Cabinet of Dr Caligari*) on the Surrealist interest in the 'cabinet of curiosities', as well as on many of Magritte's paintings. *Homage to Mack Sennett* (discussed earlier) clearly resembles the depiction of Kellar's half-open spirit cabinet, and a poster from around 1900 promoting 'Europe's Latest – De Orm's Marvelous Mysteries' depicts ghosts, devils and a nightgown-clad female spirit all emerging from a cupboard or cabinet.

Another poster from around 1915, published in Berlin by Weylandt & Bauschwitz, announces the trick of the 'Mysterious Catacombs'. The poster depicts a kind of parody of pictorial representation in which open coffins constitute picture frames containing images that come alive, the catacomb itself a kind of ghoulishly reanimated art gallery (indeed pictures are visible on the walls behind the coffins). Amid the trappings of grisly resurrection rituals (a book titled *Des Buch des Todes* (The Book of Death) lies open in the foreground), we see several open coffins containing human bodies in a variety of conditions indicated by captions – a skeleton stepping out of the coffin, corpses both fully dressed in an evening suit ('Er ist wieder belebt' – he is reanimated) and shrouded for the grave ('er stirbt' – he dies), and a skeleton with a living head, arising from the coffin ('der Kopf belebt' – the head reanimated) – an image reversed by Magritte's *The Bungler*, which depicts a female nude whose head is replaced by a skull) . The poster announces 'Experiments made with a person from the audience'. The language echoes Magritte's rhetoric of 'experimentation', which he employed (for example) in the opening remarks to his 'London Lecture', delivered as part of the 'Young Belgian Artists' exhibition at the London Gallery in March 1937: 'Ladies and Gentlemen, In the experiment we are about to make together I hope to demonstrate certain characteristics of words, images and real objects.'[15]

The proximity of magical tricks to popular Gothic tropes such as performances of clairvoyance, resurrection and spiritualist communication with the dead also influenced Magritte in significant ways. The key visual trope of skeleton/coffin, a version of the metonymic pairing of container and contained implying both death and resurrection, is adapted in a variety of ways in several paintings. *Homage to Mack Sennett* again contributes to this theme, but Magritte also produced a series of repaintings of famous works in which he replaces their protagonists with coffins. In 1949 he painted *Perspective: Manet's Balcony*, which reworks Manet's painting by replacing the human figures with coffins; and in 1950 *Perspective: David's Madame Récamier* replaces the prone female figure of David's portrait with a coffin. This painting alludes to the

René Magritte, *The Bungler*, 1935, gouache on paper.

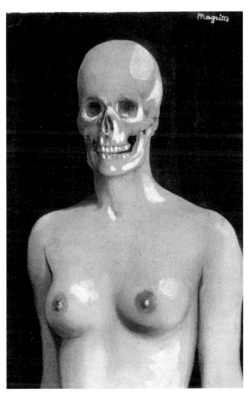

Poe-like *The Premature Burial* (1854) by the Belgian artist Antoine Wiertz, which Magritte could have seen in the Wiertz Museum in Brussels.

However, these coffin paintings also represent close iconographic relations with the magical imagery of reanimation evident in the 'Mysterious Catacombs' poster. In *Perspective: Manet's Balcony*, Magritte's casketed replacements connote the destruction or burial of the precursory artistic canon, an interpretation encouraged still further by one of the balcony figures in the original being another precursor painter, Manet's friend and sister-in-law Berthe Morisot. The balcony itself becomes in Magritte's reworking the shady place of the dead, a catacomb containing (as in the 'Mysterious

Catacombs' poster) framed paintings, miming the coffins' framing, containing and encasing of unseen bodies. The philosopher Michel Foucault, who authored works on both Magritte and Manet, made these parallels with the tomb explicit in a letter to Magritte: 'Manet's picture – particularly the window gaping onto darkness – has something of the open tomb about it.'[16]

Perspective: David's Madame Récamier is based on and partially replicates David's portrait of Madame Récamier (1800), which shows its subject reclining on a chaise longue, gazing at the viewer. She is replaced in Magritte's repainting with a coffin. In this picture Magritte is performing another kind of painterly trick, a substitution in which he implies the 'burial' of artistic tradition and traditional values, and their replacement with exhumed, posthumous versions of themselves. In an interview with Louis Quiévreux in 1947, Magritte briefly and explicitly rejects tradition itself with the words 'I hate tradition',[17] a sentiment sustained from his early interest in the artistic styles of the Italian Futurists. In their rhetoric, tradition was a monstrous oppression to be killed off and buried by the truly modern artist.[18]

The iconographic burial of Madame Récamier becomes the interment of the precursor image and its repeated resurrections in art history – David's painting was reworked as a motif by a number of artists, not least his pupils Antoine-Jean Gros (*c.* 1825) and François Gérard (the latter's version, of 1805, is also the subject of one of Magritte's repaintings). Magritte's aim is (he states) 'to reject . . . tradition', to free himself of the memory of the past.[19] He remarks, 'to be a surrealist, as I am, means barring from your mind all remembrance of what you have seen, and being always on the lookout for what has never been seen.'[20] To reject tradition and its 'remembrance' is thus implicitly to embrace novelty, or at least discover the previously overlooked. In addition, the rejection of tradition is also a rejection of the critical discourses in which it is privileged, which impose a kind of monotony of repetition in their

René Magritte, *Perspective: Manet's Balcony*, 1949, oil on canvas.

evaluation of the new against that which precedes it. As Magritte elaborated in 'Lifeline 1':

> The traditionally painterly, the only thing which was accepted by criticism, was with good reasons missing in my pictures . . . The painterly became monotonous through repetition. How can the audience look at this old church wall in sunlight or moonlight without disgust at every 'spring salon'; these onions and these eggs, once on the left of the unavoidable copperpot with its standard lamp reflexes, once on its right; or even this swan that has been prepared to copulate with thousands of Ledas since antiquity?[21]

This burial and replacement of traditional high art with the Surrealist art of the modern is effected, in Magritte's case, with the assistance of the accoutrements of contemporary mass and popular culture to be found in the magician's box of tricks.

Another version of the trope of confinement in a coffin-like container can be seen in the famous Houdiniesque painting *The Reckless Sleeper* of 1928. A figure is lying peacefully asleep in a wooden box that floats in mid-air yet is seemingly fixed at the painting's top edges; a variety of magical (and typically Magrittean) objects including an apple, a burning candle, a dove, a bow and a mirror appear to be fixed in a strange stony mass located below him. This image of a sleeper recalls posters for the illusionist Garvin ('Europe's popular magician'). In a 1926 advertisement Garvin is shown opening or closing a large box with his assistant lying inside it, demonstrating an appearance/disappearance illusion, while elsewhere in the image the assistant is depicted emerging from a transparent box.

These paintings explore the relations between image and frame and offer an extended commentary on pictorial issues of freedom and constraint, containment and escape (these being, of course,

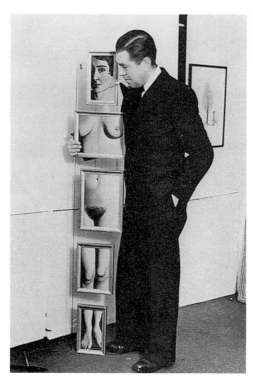

René Magritte with *The Eternally Obvious*, 1930, oil on five canvases.

popular tropes of the illusionist's performance, especially in the guise of the escapologist). These relations are also a recurrent motif, together with other stage-magic-inspired ones, in films made from 1942 onwards by Magritte and Nougé, showing themselves together with their friends enacting various, often comically imbued scenes.[22]

In *The Eternally Obvious* (1930) a life-sized model of a female nude (a portrait of Georgette) is assembled out of five separately framed paintings, a device Magritte repeated in two later paintings with different models, in a set of images commenting on and exploiting the metonymic partition of the female body in conventional nudes. The painting's illusion relies on the eye's ability to perceive the figure as complete despite its fragmentation – the dismembered

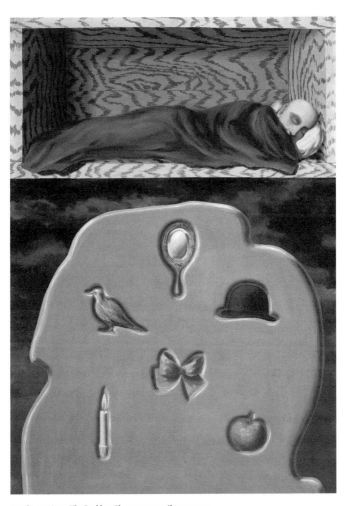

René Magritte, *The Reckless Sleeper*, 1928, oil on canvas.

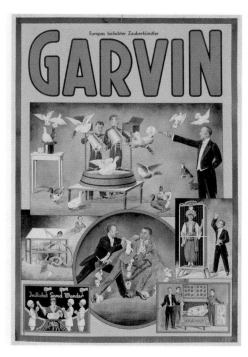

Poster advertising Garvin, 'Europe's popular magician', 1926.

body is thus reassembled in the viewer's perception, and (in a kind of spatialized version of the visual effect achieved by the cinematic process of 24-frames-per-second projection) the painting achieves its effect through presenting a kind of after-image that causes the body to be perceived as complete despite its evident fragmentation. Haim Finkelstein reads this cinematic possibility spatially, arguing that the separate frames, comprising a complete nude, emulate the 'cinematic fragmentation of a figure in separate close-ups'.[23] Magritte also plays in this painting with the Surrealist game of Exquisite Corpse, in which players add segments to a folded picture, which is then unfolded to reveal a collaborative composite image (and the possibility remains, in Magritte's painting, that the constituent parts of the nude might be rearranged in a different order).

Magritte's description of *The Eternally Obvious* relates it closely to the realm of magic. In a letter to Nougé in 1930 he describes this painting along with others executed in a similar manner:

> I have done a few objects, one of which is a naked woman and the others are a landscape and a sky. The woman is represented life-size. Each of these images is presented thus: of the woman I show only parts of the body, but situated where they should be: each of these small pictures is framed, and fixed, on a pane of glass: with a sky, or a landscape, I perform the same operation. It may be observed that with this type of picture it becomes impossible to cut them up without destroying them completely (in the case of the woman, the sky or the landscape, it seems to me that they gain from being subjected to such a process).[24]

Magritte here enacts the 'operation' of a magician, which if performed in reality would lead to the destruction of its object but which, in the field of the magical performance, actually creates it. In the magic trick 'The Aztec Lady', a magician apparently saws apart his female assistant's body in a box and then magically reassembles it. The origins of this trick are murky. Robert-Houdin mentions it in his 1858 *Memoirs*, but the first widely publicized performances of a sawing illusion were in January 1921, by the British magician P. T. Selbit at St George's Hall in London's West End and at the Finsbury Park Empire theatre. In this trick, which Selbit named (with simple literalism) 'Sawing through a Woman', his assistant, Betty Barker, was apparently locked inside a wooden crate. The illusion of her confinement in the crate was effected by ropes being tied to her hands, feet and neck, which were then held throughout the performance of the trick by audience members.

This performance recalls *The Reckless Sleeper*, but also two paintings of 1926 (both of which continue the tradition of stage imagery discussed in Chapter Two): *The Famous Man*, which shows a darkened stage with curtains framing a box containing a *bilboquet* segmented (like Georgette in *The Eternally Obvious*) into vertically arranged fragments; and *The Magician's Accomplices*, in which a female nude, framed by a red curtain to her right and a white one to her left, stands erect on a wooden stage, her raised arms, shoulders and head concealed by a golden cylinder which is suspended from above. In the foreground the arms, shoulders and head (facing away from the viewer) of another (the same?) female nude protrude above the rim of a similar cylinder, set at stage level. The date of this painting coincides with a French news article in *Le Journal amusant* on Horace Goldin's performance at the Paris Opéra music hall: 'The magician Horace Goldin shows us a series of very adroitly presented tricks. He continues to saw in two a pretty blonde who is not in too much pain.'[25] A different version of female dismemberment can be seen in a poster from 1925 advertising The Great Nicóla's trick of 'Seeing through a Woman' in which a woman remains alive while her torso is removed. *The Magician's Accomplices* is redolent of 'smoke-and-mirrors' illusionism, referring clearly to tricks in which (as the title suggests) the magician's accomplice is apparently dismembered, the separate segments of her body appearing in different places on the darkened stage.

A final magical trope commonly alluded to by Magritte is that of aerial suspension or levitation, a popular theme on posters advertising magic shows. In many of Magritte's paintings we see inanimate objects such as bells (for example *The Automaton*, 1929), apples (*The Archimedes Principle*, 1950), rocks (*The Familiar World*, 1958) or glasses and bread (*Force of Circumstances*, 1958) floating in the air; and in two versions of *The Lovers* (1928) a woman in a red dress kisses a disembodied male head suspended beside her. The second version of this painting offers another collage 'entirely painted by hand' combining a postcard image of lovers (which Magritte still owned at the time of his death) with a version of a disembodied male head depicted in a poster image of the magician

René Magritte, *The Magician's Accomplices*, 1926, oil on canvas.

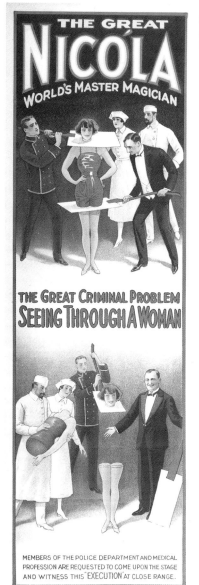

Poster for The Great Nicóla's spectacle 'Seeing Through a Woman', 1925.

'The Great Nesbitt' from about 1920, whose act used electricity to create spectacular illusions.

One of Magritte's earliest manifestations of aerial suspension can be seen in the androgynous body (corpse or dummy?) floating across the foreground of *The Musings of a Solitary Walker* (1926), a painting often associated with Magritte's Châtelet childhood and his mother's suicide.[26] Magritte largely rejected such psychoanalytic interpretations of his works, asserting that 'Psychoanalysis has . . . nothing to say about the art works which evoke the mystery of the world. Perhaps psychoanalysis is the best case for psychoanalysis to treat.'[27] Magic, on the other hand, is clearly suggested in the painting's allusion to levitation acts. It depicts a landscape, a river flowing on the left while on the right we see the back of a bowler-hatted figure – 'the ancestor of numerous other bowler-hatted men' in Magritte's work.[28] He is the archetype of the figure linking Magritte's works most closely to both cinema and circus, Charlie Chaplin, whose film *The Circus* was released in 1928 during Magritte's stay in Paris. The dark exterior setting (with the winding road and woods), the male figure and the levitating woman are all elements echoing a 1919 poster advertising the illusionist Von Arx, in which the magician, dressed in an evening suit, elevates a woman over a winding road leading through woods to a Moorish building, while Mephistopheles whispers in his ear, giving the act a whiff of the Satanic bargain.

Levitation illusions were popular in fairs and circuses, as well as in magic shows. A newspaper article from 17 August 1907 in *Le Journal amusant* illustrates the many magic spectacles at the Théâtre Marigny with a drawing of incomparable conjuror Horace Goldin levitating a woman, a staple of Goldin's programme. Between 1907 and 1914, during Magritte's childhood, Goldin regularly visited Brussels while touring Europe, receiving much newspaper attention. A 1907 *L'Indépendance Belge* article celebrating his two-week sell-out residency at the Palais d'Eté calls him

René Magritte, *The Musings of a Solitary Walker*, 1926, oil on canvas.

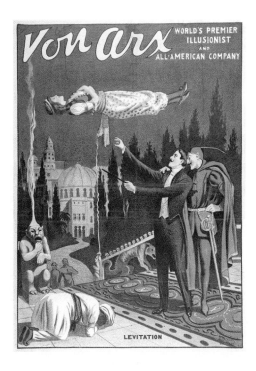

Poster for Von Arx's 'Levitation' show, 1919.

'Le roi des magiciens' (the king of magicians),[29] and another from April 1909 describes him as a 'futuriste' who has taken over the reign and carries forward the legacy of Herrmann the Great and Robert-Houdin, and announces his upcoming performances: 'It is a fact that his reputation is not foreign to Brussels.'[30] An article in the *Gazette de Charleroi* of 8 June 1913 announces the arrival of 'The most marvellous illusionist – together with his sixty collaborators and his tigers – for shows at the Bruxelles Théâtre Music-Hall in the Luna Park.[31] Matinée performances reserved for families were an important part of the success of these magicians, and wealthier children from Brussels and its vicinities, like Magritte, would certainly have attended them.

Georgette, Finally

The little girl I had known in the cemetery was the
object of my daydreams and was caught in the exciting
atmosphere of train stations, fairs or towns that I created
for her. Thanks to that magical painting I rediscovered
the feelings I had experienced in my childhood.[32]

Histories of stage magic often overlook the fact that most
magicians work with accomplices and assistants (and art histories
have similarly repressed or simply omitted the collaborative input
of female partners to the works of male artists, constructing them
instead as muses who inspire passively, but contribute little else
to, the man's works). Georgette Magritte's contribution to creating
many of her partner's works has likewise been largely overlooked
by critics. She is mostly represented as marginal to Magritte's
productivity, yet her role as a partner in life and in the business
of artistic creativity, as an actively involved contributor to the
production of works, is significant. Georgette's extensive work
with Magritte is particularly visible when viewed in relation to the
significance of stage magic and prestidigitation in his works, which
enables us to see her not simply as a loyal wife but as a crucial and
active professional partner contributing fully to the conception,
performance and effects of Magritte's painterly magic tricks.

   Traditionally the relations between model and artist are
presented as hierarchical, the artist/model dichotomy reproducing
the conventional male/female stereotype of active/passive,
controlling/controlled, creator/created (and Magritte's *Attempting
the Impossible* is interesting in this context). Yet, Georgette's
prominence as figure and subject in Magritte's paintings indicates
the closeness of their professional relationship. She posed for most
of Magritte's nudes, and from 1923 he continued to portray her
throughout his career. Her insistent presence as figure in these

paintings suggests that we might understand her contribution to Magritte's aesthetic productivity as resembling that of the magician's assistant – a significant performative role in itself, and a crucial part of the magic act.

Georgette first appears in this role in *Reclining Nude* of 1928, where her stiff posture and staring gaze evoke stage-magic acts using hypnotism, while a variety of objects are balanced like performance props on her body. This painting's allusions to representations of magic acts are reinforced by its historical proximity to *Attempting the Impossible*, painted soon after, which depicts Georgette as the assistant who plays the materializing figure in the image's riff on the 'Pepper's Ghost Effect' illusion. This materialization/dematerialization trope returns in many representations of her figure dissolving into seascapes in the background, as is the case in paintings like *Black Magic* (discussed earlier, see p. 107) and *The Universal Mirror* (1938–9).

Georgette's role as the magician's assistant and accomplice is also visually established by images Magritte produced from the early 1940s onwards representing her posing with doves. In a second version of *The Break in the Clouds* (1942) she appears nude, looking at a dove landing on her left hand while holding what seems to be a ball or an egg in her right. Her environment is that of the magician's stage – heavy curtains on the left and a burning fire accompany her pose. In a 1938 photograph of Georgette by Magritte titled *Le Rendez-vous*, she sits with crossed arms holding two doves, as if presenting them to us as part of a magic act, and in a photograph of 1947 she is shown in profile, offering the audience a leaf and a glass of water, props of a conjuring trick, a small spillage from the glass disrupting the otherwise perfectly posed and composed scene, like a deliberate but inconsequential error to misdirect the viewer.

The visual device of the magician with his accoutrements suspended in the air around him can be seen in many posters

René Magritte,
Le Rendez-vous
(Georgette Magritte,
Brussels), 1938,
photograph.

advertising magic acts. A poster for 'Brush the Mystic' from 1920
represents said mystic surrounded by floating roses, playing cards,
doves and a multitude of other objects that swirl mysteriously at his
apparent command from the genie's lamp in front of him. Magritte
adapted this familiar trope in several portraits of Georgette,
implying she takes the position of the magician in their creative
partnership. *Georgette* (1935) shows her disembodied head as double
– face-on and in profile – suspended before a tiled wall with, on
her right, a window opening on to a seascape. Objects associated
with conjuring acts of disappearance and displacement, and with
the devices of the seance, float around the portrait at the margins
of the picture frame – key, egg, olive branch, a glove, an envelope
and a candle illuminating her face. The 1937 version pictured here
portrays her in a style clearly resembling that used in magic posters
of the time, now as a single head and neck in the more conventional

René Magritte, *Georgette*, 1937, oil on canvas.

setting of an internal frame resembling a locket portrait or a mirror image, surrounded by a similar collection of objects – dove, key, candle, glove, olive branch, a piece of paper with the word '*vague*' (wave) written upon it.

This version was captured in Duane Michals's photoshoot with the Magrittes in their house on rue des Mimosas in August 1965, two years before Magritte's death. Magritte is dressed in a bowler hat and suit and is opening the door, his figure framed by the various window and door frames that multiply in the picture, while the simple 'MAGRITTE' next to his doorbell suggests a signature inscription, as if Magritte had authorized the image himself. The juxtaposition of the portrait of Georgette within the frame with the banal, domestic setting she inhabits outside of it sets up a now familiar series of tensions between the subversive potentials of Magritte's Surrealist experiments and the restricted, conventional bourgeois domestic context. Michals's photographs play with Magritte's image as a magician; across the shoot he both appears and remains curiously invisible, multiplying himself in reflections, playing with his hat in an Oliver Hardyesque manner (sometimes it sits upside down atop his head), while Georgette's pearls and formal dress evoke her impersonation of the Magrittean bourgeois camouflage, her pose and look echoing her detached manner in *Reclining Nude*. These qualities have the effect of her positioning herself as part of the act. Michals writes at the end of the published collection of her photographs: 'Dedicated to Georgette Magritte, the woman who shared René Magritte's life and whose graciousness made this book possible.'[33] One of Michals's photographs seems eerily to prefigure the artist's death by depicting René Magritte asleep as if he had disappeared already into the image of himself that his corpse would later present – while simultaneously alluding back to *The Reckless Sleeper* of 1928.

Returning from a short hospitalization, Magritte died at the age of 68 in his home at 97 rue des Mimosas on 15 August 1967, after a

Duane Michals, *René Magritte Asleep*, 1965, photograph.

long illness. He had been diagnosed with pancreatic cancer in 1963
and underwent exploratory surgery in 1965, but was well enough
that December to travel with Georgette and their dog Loulou to
New York, his only visit to America, for the retrospective of his
work at MOMA. While there, the Magrittes visited Edgar Allan Poe's
cottage in the Bronx ('Poe's house is the finest in the USA. We were
welcomed by a raven on top of a narrow cupboard,' he wrote to
Scutenaire[34]). They also travelled south to visit the collectors Jean
and Dominique de Menil in Houston, where Magritte also attended
a rodeo. According to Georgette, the city of Brussels approached
Magritte shortly before his death, hoping to rename rue des
Mimosas after him, but he refused them permission. He is buried
in the cemetery at Schaerbeek. Georgette died in 1986 and is buried
with him. Their grave marker bears simply their names and dates.

The fairground, its carousels and attractions, the circus ring,
the cinematic screen and its projections, the camera obscura and
panorama, and the worlds of conjuring and illusions are all key
aspects of Magritte's childhood, together comprising integral

and formative elements of his artistic production. All along
these enticing carnivalesque worlds stood, clearly visible, in the
biographical images of the fairground ride, and subsequently in
their different manifestations and permutations across Magritte's
oeuvre and personae, presented to us by the artist himself – like
a conjuror performing and simultaneously, unbeknown to the
audience, revealing the secret of his trick – in his autobiographical
allusions to the place du Manège.

References

Introduction: 'Meet me at the carousel!'

1 Pierre Souvestre and Marcel Allain, 'Juve against Fantômas', in *The Fantômas Megapack* (Rockville, MD, 2016), p. 402.
2 René Magritte interviewed by Carl Waï, 20 January 1967, in *René Magritte: Selected Writings*, ed. Kathleen Rooney and Eric Plattner, trans. Jo Levy (Richmond, 2016), p. 231.
3 *Catalogue Raisonné* references are to the following texts and abbreviated CR I, CR II and CR III:
   David Sylvester and Sarah Whitfield, eds, *René Magritte, Catalogue Raisonné I: Oil Paintings, 1916–1930* (Houston, TX, and London, 1992).
   David Sylvester and Sarah Whitfield, eds, *René Magritte, Catalogue Raisonné II: Oil Paintings and Objects, 1931–1948* (Antwerp, 1993).
   David Sylvester and Sarah Whitfield, eds, *Catalogue Raisonné III: Oil Paintings, Objects and Bronzes, 1949–1967* (London, 1993).
4 George Melly, 'Robbing Banks', *London Review of Books*, XIV/12 (25 June 1992), pp. 7–8.
5 James Thrall Soby, *René Magritte* (New York, 1965), p. 7.
6 *CR I*, p. 3.
7 Ibid., p. 5. Sylvester and Whitfield note the company as Maggic, but this seems to be a misprint.
8 *La Région de Charleroi* (27 October 1916), p. 3. All translations author's own.
9 *Journal de Charleroi* (14 August 1906), p. 3. All translations author's own.
10 *CR I*, p. 5.
11 Ibid., p. 8.
12 *Gazette de Charleroi* (13 March 1912), p. 3. All translations author's own.
13 *CR I*, p. 10.

14 Ibid., p. 7.

15 Ibid.

16 Ellen Handler Spitz, *Museums of the Mind* (London, 1994), p. 41.

17 René Magritte, 'Autobiographical Sketch' [1954], in *René Magritte*, ed. Rooney and Plattner, p. 151.

18 Ibid., p. 10.

19 Michel Draguet, *Magritte* (Paris, 2014).

20 *Gazette de Charleroi* (14 August 1904), p. 2.

21 Philippe Dimbourg, *La Foire autrefois en Wallonie et à Bruxelles* (Brussels, 2005), p. 92.

22 *Gazette de Charleroi* (9 January 1913), p. 4.

23 Guido Convents, 'Motion Picture Exhibitors on Belgian Fairgrounds: Unknown Aspects of Travelling Exhibition in a European Country, 1896–1914', *Film History*, vi (1994), p. 238.

24 Ibid.

25 See ibid.

26 David Sylvester, *Magritte* (London, 1992), p. 9.

27 René Magritte, 'Lifeline i' [1938], in *René Magritte*, ed. Rooney and Plattner, pp. 58–67: p. 58.

1 Independent Beginnings: Shaping Belgian Surrealism

1 *CR i*, p. 11.

2 Ibid., p. 14.

3 David Sylvester, *Magritte* (London, 1992), p. 32.

4 E.L.T. Mesens, 'Autour de René Magritte', in *CR i*, p. 20.

5 *CR i*, p. 21.

6 Gérard Durozoi, *History of the Surrealist Movement* (London, 2002), p. 147.

7 *CR i*, p. 47.

8 René Magritte, letter to Phil Mertens, 23 February 1967, in *CR i*, p. 21.

9 Mesens, 'Autour de René Magritte', pp. 21–2.

10 René Magritte, 'Esquisse autobiographique' [1954], in *René Magritte: Écrits Complets*, ed. André Blavier (Paris, 2001), pp. 366–8: p. 367.

11 E.L.T. Mesens, 'René Magritte', in *Peintres belges contemporains*, 81 (1947), p. 158.

12 *CR I*, p. 39.

13 Ibid.

14 E.L.T. Mesens, quoted in Dawn Ades, *Dada and Surrealism Reviewed* (London, 1978), p. 331.

15 Gisèle Ollinger-Zinque, 'Introduction', trans. Jacques J. Halber, in *The Belgian Contribution to Surrealism*, exh. cat., Royal Scottish Academy (Edinburgh, 1971), pp. 6–13: p. 8.

16 José Vovelle, *Le surréalisme en Belgique* (Paris, 1972), p. 15.

17 Roger Rothman, 'Against Sincerity: René Magritte, Paul Nougé and the Lesson of Paul Valéry', *Word and Image*, XXIII/3 (September 2007), pp. 304–14: p. 305.

18 André Breton, 'Manifesto of Surrealism' [1924], in *Manifestoes of Surrealism*, trans. Richard Seaver and Helen R. Lane (Ann Arbor, MI, 1972), p. 30.

19 Rothman, 'Against Sincerity', p. 305.

20 Ibid., p. 306.

21 Ibid.

22 Valéry, cited ibid.

23 André Breton, 'Second Manifesto of Surrealism' [1929–30], in *Manifestoes of Surrealism*, p. 160.

24 Simon Dell, 'Love and Surrealism: René Magritte and André Breton in 1929', *Word and Image*, XIX/3 (July–September 2003), pp. 214–22: p. 217.

25 René Magritte, 'Words and Images' [1929], in *René Magritte: Selected Writings*, ed. Kathleen Rooney and Eric Plattner, trans. Jo Levy (Richmond, 2016), p. 33.

26 Marcel Mariën, 'Der Surrealismus aus Brüsseler Sicht', in Kunstverein und Kunsthaus Hamburg, *René Magritte und der Surrealismus in Belgien* (Brussels, 1982), p. 20.

27 André Souris, 'Paul Nougé et ses complices', in *Entretiens sur le surréalisme*, ed. Ferdinand Alquié (Paris, 1968), pp. 432–54: p. 445.

28 See J. H. Matthews, 'Marcel Mariën: Review', *L'Activité surréaliste en Belgique, Symposium: A Quarterly Journal in Modern Literatures*, XXXIV/2 (1980), p. 180.

29 André Breton, 'What is Surrealism?' [1934], in *What is Surrealism? Selected Writings*, ed. Franklin Rosemont (London, 1978), p. 112.

30 Matthews, 'Marcel Mariën', p. 180.

31 *CR II*, p. 147.

32 Ibid.

33 Paul Nougé, 'Les Points sur les signes' [1948], in Nougé, *Histoire de ne pas rire* (Lausanne, 1980), pp. 284–5.

34 André Breton, 'Surrealism and Painting' [1928], in Breton, *Surrealism and Painting*, trans. Simon Watson Taylor (London, 1972), pp. 1–48: p. 1.

35 Ibid.

36 Ibid., pp. 84–5.

37 Harry Torczyner, *Magritte: Zeichen und Bilder*, trans. Christiane Müller (Cologne, 1977), p. 59.

38 Paul Nougé, 'La Conférence de Charleroi', in Nougé, *Histoire de ne pas rire*, pp. 171–5.

2 From Commerce to Art

1 René Magritte, 'Esquisse autobiographique' [1954], in *René Magritte: Écrits Complets*, ed. André Blavier (Paris, 2001), pp. 366–8: p. 367.

2 René Magritte, undated letter to Pierre Flouquet, cited in David Sylvester, *Magritte* (London, 1992), p. 45.

3 *CR I*, p. 30.

4 Ibid.

5 Ibid., p. 43.

6 Ibid., p. 44.

7 See Nele Bernheim, 'Couture Norine: Avant-garde Belgian Fashion, 1918–1952', MA dissertation, SUNY Fashion Institute for Technology, New York, 2015, p. 15.

8 *CR I*, p. 43.

9 *Gazette de Charleroi* (12 May 1901), p. 3.

10 *Gazette de Charleroi* (16 December 1913), p. 3.

11 *Gazette de Charleroi* (19 April 1913), p. 4.

12 See poster 'Der Grosze Circus De Jonghe', *Europeana Collections*, www.europeana.eu, accessed 9 December 2017.

13 Pierre Bost, *Le Cirque et le music-hall* (Paris, 1931), p. 101.

14 *CR I*, p. 157.

15 Ibid.

16 Sarah Whitfield, *Magritte* (London, 1992), p. 154.

17 *CR II*, p. 259.

18 Ibid.

19 Ibid.

20 *CR I*, p. 170; Nathalia Brodskaïa, *Surrealism* (New York, 2012), p. 175.

21 Magritte, 'Esquisse autobiographique', p. 368.

22 'Magritte Interviewed by Jacques Goossens' (18 January 1966), in *René Magritte: Selected Writings*, ed. Kathleen Rooney and Eric Plattner, trans. Jo Levy (Richmond, 2016), pp. 217–22: p. 218.

23 Ibid., p. 219 ('considered worthwhile'); *CR I*, p. 170.

24 Camille Goemans, 'La Jeune Peinture belge', *Bulletin de la vie artistique* (1 September 1926), p. 269.

25 Paul-Gustave Van Hecke, 'René Magritte: peintre de la pensée abstraite', *Sélection* (March 1927), pp. 439–44: p. 442.

26 Brodskaïa, *Surrealism*, p. 175.

27 *CR I*, p. 170.

28 See ibid.

29 Patricia Allmer, *René Magritte: Beyond Painting* (Manchester, 2009), p. 218.

30 See ibid.

31 See Paul Augé, *Larousse du xxe siècle*, 6 vols (Paris, *c*. 1928–33), vol. i: *A–Carl*; vol. ii: *Carm–D*; vol. iii: *E–H*; vol. iv: *I–M*; vol. v: *N–Riz*; vol. vi: *Ro–Z*.

32 See Philippe Dimbourg, *La Foire autrefois en Wallonie et à Bruxelles* (Brussels, 2005), p. 92.

33 Ibid.

34 Bost, *Le Cirque et le music-hall*, p. 101.

35 The libretto can be found at https://gsarchive.net/british/gottenberg/index.html, accessed 4 February 2019.

36 *Le Peuple* (4 June 1914), p. 1.

37 *L'Indépendance Belge* (1 February 1894), p. 3. All translations author's own.

3   Going to the Pictures

1   Robert Short, 'Magritte and the Cinema', in *Surrealism: Surrealist Visuality*, ed. Silvano Levy (New York, 1997), pp. 95–108: p. 101.

2   Michel Draguet, *Magritte* (Paris, 2014), p. 32.

3   Guido Convents, 'Motion Picture Exhibitors on Belgian Fairgrounds: Unknown Aspects of Travelling Exhibition in a European Country, 1896–1914', *Film History*, vi (1994), pp. 238–49: p. 239.

4 Haim Finkelstein, *The Screen in Surrealist Art and Thought* (Aldershot and Burlington, VT, 2007), p. 161.

5 Ibid.

6 Convents, 'Motion Picture Exhibitors', p. 237.

7 *Gazette de Charleroi* (24 October 1912), p. 1.

8 *Gazette de Charleroi* (1 April 1912), p. 1.

9 *Gazette de Charleroi* (31 December 1911), p. 1.

10 *Gazette de Charleroi* (3 March 1912), p. 1; (29 May 1912), p. 1; (4 February 1913), p. 1.

11 *Gazette de Charleroi* (23 February 1913), p. 1.

12 *Gazette de Charleroi* (22 November 1913), p. 1.

13 Leen Engelen, 'Film/Cinema (Belgium)', https://encyclopedia.1914-1918-online.net (8 October 2014).

14 Ibid.

15 Ibid.

16 *La Région de Charleroi* (7 November 1915), p. 2.

17 *La Région de Charleroi* (30 October 1915), p. 2.

18 *La Région de Charleroi* (8 July 1916), p. 2.

19 *La Région de Charleroi* (18 November 1916), p. 2.

20 *Le Bruxellois* (9 December 1915), p. 2.

21 René Magritte, 'Nat Pinkerton' [1953], in *René Magritte: Selected Writings*, ed. Kathleen Rooney and Eric Plattner, trans. Jo Levy (Richmond, 2016), p. 144.

22 Fredric Jameson, 'Real Qualities of the Microcosm: Raymond Chandler in Los Angeles, USA', www.versobooks.com (25 August 2016).

23 'Magritte Interviewed by Jacques Goossens' (18 January 1966), in *René Magritte*, ed. Rooney and Plattner, p. 217.

24 Paul Éluard, 'René Magritte', *Cahiers d'Art*, vols V–VI (1935), pp. 130–31.

25 *CR I*, p. 111.

26 Marcel Allain and Pierre Souvestre, *Fantômas*, trans. Cranstoun Metcalfe (London, 1986), p. 7.

27 *Le Peuple* (11 October 1913), p. 4.

28 *CR I*, p. 164.

29 Ibid., p. 209.

30 Laura Rosenstock, 'De Chirico's Influence on the Surrealists', in *De Chirico*, ed. William Rubin (New York, 1982), pp. 111–30: p. 120.

31 *CR I*, p. 209.

32 Max Ernst, 'Some Data on the Youth of M. E.' [1942], trans. Dorothea
     Tanning, in *Max Ernst: Beyond Painting and Other Writings by the Artist
     and his Friends*, ed. Robert Motherwell (New York, 1948), p. 17.
33 Finkelstein, *The Screen in Surrealist Art and Thought*, p. 164.
34 René Magritte, letter to André Bosmans, 30 September 1959, in
     René Magritte: Écrits Complets, ed. André Blavier (Paris, 2001), p. 500.
35 Blavier, 'Magritte et le cinéma', in *René Magritte*, ed. Blavier,
     pp. 500–503.
36 Ibid. For a discussion of resonances between Magritte and Hitchcock's
     work see Patricia Allmer, 'Dial "M" for Magritte', in *Johan Grimonprez:
     Looking for Alfred*, ed. Steven Bode and Thomas Elsaesser (London,
     2007), pp. 208–23.
37 René Magritte, interview with Jean Neyens [1965], in *René Magritte*, ed.
     Blavier, p. 605.
38 See Patricia Allmer, 'Framing the Real: Frames and the Processes of
     Framing in René Magritte's Oeuvre', in *Framing Borders in Literature
     and Other Media*, ed. Werner Wolf and Walter Bernhart (Amsterdam
     and New York, 2006), pp. 113–38.
39 *CR I*, p. 275.
40 Joan M. Minguet Batllori, 'Buñuel, Dalí y *Un Chien andalou* (1929): el
     enredo de la creación', *Archivos de la Filmoteca*, 37 (February 2001),
     pp. 6–19: p. 16.
41 Ibid., pp. 16–17.
42 *CR I*, p. 105.
43 Paul Hammond, 'Available Light', in *The Shadow and its Shadow:
     Surrealist Writings on the Cinema*, ed. Paul Hammond (San Francisco,
     CA, 2000), p. 13.
44 See Gilles Deleuze, *Cinema 1: The Movement-image*, trans. Hugh
     Tomlinson and Barbara Habberjam (London, 2005).

4 From Camera Obscura to Panoramic Vision

1 *CR II*, p. 176.
2 Ibid., p. 184.
3 René Magritte, letter to Felix Fabrizio, 3 September 1966, in Sarah
     Whitfield, *Magritte* (London, 1992), p. 141.

4 René Magritte, 'La Ligne de vie I' [1938], in *René Magritte Écrits Complets*, ed. André Blavier (Paris, 2001), p. 111.

5 Plato, *The Allegory of the Cave*, in *The Republic* (Book VII), trans. Benjamin Jowett (Los Angeles, CA, 2017), p. 9.

6 David Sylvester, 'Handwritten List and Notes of Magritte's Library', BDF C04, courtesy of Menil Archives, The Menil Collection, Houston, TX.

7 René Magritte, letter to Paul Éluard, December 1935, in *CR II*, p. 213.

8 Alexander Iolas, letter to René Magritte, 15 October 1952, in *CR III*, p. 192.

9 René Magritte, letter to Alexander Iolas, 24 October 1952, in *CR III*, p. 192.

10 Guido Convents, 'Motion Picture Exhibitors on Belgian Fairgrounds: Unknown Aspects of Travelling Exhibition in a European Country, 1896–1914', *Film History*, VI (1914), pp. 238–49: p. 239.

11 *Le Soir* (3 April 1911), p. 3.

12 *CR I*, p. 7.

13 Ibid., p. 12.

14 'La Seconde Exposition universelle de Liège', *La Meuse* (24 October 1910), p. 2. All translations author's own.

15 Keith M. Johnston, *Science Fiction Film: A Critical Introduction* (London, 2011), p. 43.

16 Visitor comment at www.worldfairs.info, accessed 9 December 2017.

17 Ibid.

18 *Exposition universelle et international*, exh. cat. (Ghent, 1913), n.p.

19 Tom Gunning, 'The World as Object Lesson: Cinema Audiences, Visual Culture and the St Louis World's Fair, 1904', *Film History*, VI/4 (Winter 1994), pp. 422–44.

20 *Gazette de Charleroi* (6 August 1908), p. 3.

21 Ibid.

22 *La Meuse* (5 November 1910), p. 2.

23 *Journal de Charleroi* (19 November 1905), p. 4.

24 Shelley Rice, 'Boundless Horizons: The Panoramic Image', *Art in America*, LXXXI (1993), pp. 68–71: p. 70.

25 Sigmund Freud, *Die Traumdeutung* (Leipzig and Vienna, 1914), p. 246.

26 *CR III*, p. 354.

27 William Uricchio, 'A "Proper Point of View": The Panorama and Some of Its Early Media Iterations', *Early Popular Visual Culture*, IX/3

(September 2011), pp. 225–38; p. 228, at http://web.mit.edu, accessed 9 December 2017.

28 *CR III*, pp. 321–2.

29 Alison Griffiths, *Shivers Down Your Spine: Cinema, Museums, and the Immersive View* (New York, 2013), pp. 5, 6.

30 *CR III*, p. 189.

31 Ibid.

32 Ibid., p. 25.

33 Ibid., p. 40.

34 René Magritte, letter to Louis Scutenaire and Irène Hamoir, 4 June 1953, in *CR III*, p. 42.

35 Conseil Communal de la Ville de Charleroi, letter to René Magritte, 28 March 1956, in *CR III*, p. 65.

36 René Magritte, letter to Maurice and Dors Rapin, 15 June 1956, in *CR III*, p. 255.

5 Subversive Allegiances

1 René Magritte, 'René Magritte and the Communist Party, 2: From a Letter to the Communist Party of Belgium', in *René Magritte: Selected Writings*, ed. Kathleen Rooney and Eric Plattner, trans. Jo Levy (Richmond, 2016), p. 105.

2 René Magritte, 'Life Line 1' [1938], in *René Magritte*, ed. Rooney and Plattner , p. 58.

3 Ibid., p. 62.

4 René Magritte and Louis Scutenaire, 'Bourgeois Art', *London Bulletin*, 12 (15 March 1939), pp. 13–14.

5 André Blavier, ed., *René Magritte: Écrits Complets* (Paris, 2001), p. 248.

6 Patrick Waldberg, *René Magritte* (Brussels, 1965), p. 208.

7 Magritte 'Life Line 1', p. 62.

8 Magritte, 'Magritte and the Communist Party, 2', p. 105.

9 Bob Claessens (October 1947), quoted in *René Magritte*, ed. Blavier, pp. 243–4.

10 René Magritte, 'Magritte and the Communist Party, 2', p. 106.

11 René Magritte, 'Magritte and the Communist Party, 3: Letter to *Le Drapeau rouge*', in *René Magritte*, ed. Rooney and Plattner, p. 107.

12 Blavier, ed., *René Magritte*, pp. 247–8.

13 René Magritte, interview with Jean Neyens [1965], quoted ibid., p. 239.

14 See Marcel Mariën, *Le Radeau de la mémoire: Souvenirs déterminés* (1983), pp. 101–4.

15 *CR II*, pp. 99–100 (questionable provenance); Patricia Allmer, *René Magritte: Beyond Painting* (Manchester, 2009), p. 75 (forged by himself).

16 *CR III*, p. 119.

17 Ibid.

18 Ibid.

19 Ibid., p. 67.

20 'Hodes, Barnet', René Magritte, letter to Barnet Hodes, 8 April 1960, MC [03] III/03, courtesy of Menil Archives, The Menil Collection, Houston, TX.

21 Quoted in George Melly, 'Robbing Banks', *London Review of Books*, XIV/12 (25 June 1992), pp. 7–8.

22 Allmer, *René Magritte: Beyond Painting*, p. 8.

23 'Magritte's Speech on Being Elected as a Member of the Académie Picard', in *René Magritte*, ed. Rooney and Plattner, pp. 173–4: p. 174.

24 *CR III*, p. 75.

25 *Gazette de Charleroi* (20 March 1913), p. 3.

26 Richard Calvocoressi, *Magritte* (London, 1998), p. 100.

27 Maurice Nadeau, *The History of Surrealism* [1944], trans. Richard Howard (Cambridge, MA, 1989), p. 156.

28 Dawn Ades and Fiona Bradley, 'Introduction', in *Undercover Surrealism: Georges Bataille and Documents*, ed. Dawn Ades and Simon Baker (Cambridge, MA, 2006), p. 11.

29 Linda M. Steer, 'Photographic Appropriation: Ethnography and the Surrealist Other', *The Comparatist*, 32 (May 2008), p. 72.

30 Michel Leiris, 'De Bataille l'impossible à l'impossible *Documents*', *Critique*, 195–6: special issue 'Hommage à Georges Bataille' (August–September 1963), p. 689.

31 Michael Richardson, 'Introduction' to Georges Bataille, *The Absence of Myth: Writings on Surrealism* (London, 1994), p. 11.

32 *CR II*, p. 113.

33 *CR III*, pp. 94, 316; *CR II*, p. 316.

34 Patrick Waldberg, *René Magritte* (Brussels, 1965), p. 156.

35 Georges Bataille, letter to René Magritte, 26 July 1960, MC [02] II/03 Magritte Correspondence, courtesy of the Menil Foundation.

36 Georges Bataille, letter to René Magritte, 2 March 1961, MC [02] II/03 Magritte Correspondence, courtesy of the Menil Foundation.

37 Calvocoressi, *Magritte*, p. 100.

38 Christoph Grunenberg, 'Bataille', in *Magritte, A to Z*, ed. Christoph Grunenberg and Darren Pih (Liverpool, 2011), n.p.

39 Ibid.

40 Marcel Mariën, 'Dans un sépulcre près de la mer', *Les lèvres nues*, 1 (January 1969), n.p.

41 Louis Scutenaire, *Avec Magritte* (Brussels, 1977), p. 111.

42 Denys Chevalier, in *CR II*, p. 165.

43 Ibid.

44 Ibid., p. 154.

45 Ibid., p. 132.

46 André Breton, *Free Rein* (*La Clé des champs*), trans. Michel Parmentier and Jacqueline d'Amboise (Lincoln, NE, and London, 1995), p. 282.

47 René Magritte, *Idiot, Silly Bugger* and *Fucker*, in *René Magritte*, ed. Rooney and Plattner, pp. 76–8.

48 Ibid., pp. 76, 78.

49 Georges Bataille, *Madame Edwarda*, in Bataille, *My Mother/Madame Edwarda/The Dead Man*, trans. Austryn Wainhouse (London and New York, 1989), p. 154.

50 Ibid., p. 156.

51 Ibid., p. 150.

52 Georges Bataille, 'Preface' to *Madame Edwarda*, p. 139.

53 Georges Bataille, *The Tears of Eros* [1961], trans. Peter Connor (San Francisco, CA, 1989), p. 177.

54 Georges Bataille, 'Laughter', in *The Bataille Reader*, ed. Fred Botting and Scott Wilson (Oxford, 1997), pp. 59–63: p. 62.

55 Mikhail Bakhtin, *Rabelais and his World*, trans. Hélène Iswolsky (Bloomington, IN, 2009), p. 66.

6 Now You See Him, Now You Don't . . .

1 Colin Williamson, *Hidden in Plain Sight: An Archaeology of Magic and the Cinema* (New Brunswick, NJ, 2015), p. 12.
2 René Gaffé, 'Magritte, René', in *The Enchanted Domain* (Exeter, 1967), n.p.; Marina Warner, *Phantasmagoria: Spirit Visions, Metaphors, and Media into the Twenty-first Century* (Oxford, 2006), p. 321.
3 *La Meuse* (5 June 1909), p. 2.
4 *La Meuse* (18 December 1909), p. 3.
5 *Le Soir* (8 June 1913), p. 1.
6 *Journal de Charleroi* (29 May 1906), p. 3.
7 *Journal de Charleroi* (19 January 1914), p. 1.
8 Gabe Fajuri and Stina Henslee, *The Golden Age of Magic Posters: The Nielsen Collection, Part II*, Potter & Potter Auctions, 4 February 2017, p. 5.
9 *Paris-soir* (18 June 1927), p. 2.
10 Lynda Nead, *The Haunted Gallery: Painting, Photography, Film, c. 1900* (New Haven, CT, 2007), p. 101.
11 *CR I*, p. 268.
12 René Magritte, 'La Ligne de vie I' [1938], in *René Magritte: Écrits Complets*, ed. André Blavier (Paris, 2001), p. 109.
13 Ibid., p. 110.
14 René Magritte, letter to Ferdinand Alquié, 11 June 1959, in *René Magritte*, ed. Blavier, p. 448.
15 René Magritte, letter to Marcel Duchamp, 1966, in *René Magritte*, ed. Blavier, p. 377.
16 Giuseppe Pinetti, *The Conjuror's Repository; or, The Whole Art and Mystery of Magic Displayed by the Following Celebrated Characters: Pinetti, Katterfelto, Barret, Brislaw, Sibley, Lane & Co.* (London, 1793), p. 22.
17 René Magritte, 'Leçon de choses: Ecrits et dessins de René Magritte', *Rhétorique*, 7 (October 1962), n.p.
18 Christopher Priest, *The Prestige* (London, 1995), pp. 64–5.
19 R. Bruce Elder, *Dada, Surrealism, and the Cinematic Effect* (Waterloo, ON, 2015), p. 495.
20 Arthur Good, *100 Amazing Magic Tricks*, trans. and adapted by David Roberts and Cliff Andrew (London, 1977), p. 85.
21 Ibid.

22　See Jacques Lacan, 'The Mirror Stage', in *Écrits*, trans. Bruce Fink (New York, 2006), pp. 75–81.

23　*CR II*, p. 244.

24　Michel Draguet, *Magritte* (Paris, 2014), p. 24.

25　Magritte, 'La Ligne de vie I', p. 105.

26　René Magritte, 'La Ligne de vie II', in *René Magritte*, ed. Blavier, p. 142.

27　René Magritte, 'Words of René Magritte', in *Secret Affinities: Words and Images by René Magritte*, trans. W. G. Rya, exh. cat., Institute for the Arts, Rice University (Houston, TX, 1976), p. 3.

28　Magritte, 'La Ligne de vie I', p. 105.

29　Ibid., p. 110.

30　Ibid., p. 111.

31　Patricia Allmer, *René Magritte: Beyond Painting* (Manchester, 2009), p. 206.

32　Pinetti, *The Conjuror's Repository*, p. 22.

33　Magritte, 'Leçon de choses', n.p.

34　René Magritte, 'René Magritte et le cinéma' (interview with Jacques de Decker), *Entr'acte*, 1 (October 1960), p. 13; also in Blavier, ed., *René Magritte*, p. 498.

35　*Paris-soir* (18 June 1927), p. 2.

7　Disappearing Acts

1　See Ainsley Brown, 'René Magritte and Paul Éluard: An International and Interartistic Dialogue', *Image [&] Narrative*, issue 13: *The Forgotten Surrealists: Belgian Surrealism since 1924*, ed. Patricia Allmer and Hilde Van Gelder (2005), www.imageandnarrative.be, accessed 4 April 2018.

2　*CR III*, p. 59.

3　Ibid., p. 60.

4　George Melly, 'The World According to Magritte', *Sphere* (January–February 1985), p. 14.

5　*CR III*, p. 85.

6　'Magritte Interviewed by Jacques Goossens (18 January 1966)', in *René Magritte: Selected Writings*, ed. Kathleen Rooney and Eric Plattner, trans. Jo Levy (Richmond, 2016), p. 217.

7 René Magritte, 'A Judgement on Art' [1957], in *René Magritte*, ed. Rooney and Plattner, p. 175.

8 René Magritte, 'Interview Jean Neyens' [1965], in *René Magritte: Écrits Complets*, ed. André Blavier (Paris, 2001), p. 603.

9 Matthieu Letourneux, 'The Magician's Box of Tricks: Fantômas, Popular Literature, and the Spectacular Imagination', in *Sensationalism and The Genealogy of Modernity: A Global Nineteenth-century Perspective*, ed. Alberto Gabriele (Basingstoke, 2017), pp. 143–62: p. 154.

10 *Paris-soir* (18 June 1927), p. 2.

11 *CR I*, p. 250.

12 René Magritte, letter to Paul Nougé, November 1927, in *CR I*, p. 246.

13 Marcel Paquet, *René Magritte, 1898–1967* (San Diego, CA, 1997), p. 61.

14 Catherine Hindson, 'The Female Illusionist: Loïe Fuller, Fairy or Wizardess?', *Early Popular Visual Culture*, IV/2 (May 2006), pp. 161–74: p. 170.

15 René Magritte, 'London Lecture' [1937], in *René Magritte*, ed. Rooney and Plattner, pp. 51–5: p. 54.

16 *CR III*, p. 146.

17 René Magritte, interview in *Time* (21 April 1947), pp. 75–6; also in Blavier, ed., *René Magritte*, p. 251.

18 Filippo Tommaso Marinetti, 'The Foundation and Manifesto of Futurism' [1909], in *Art in Theory, 1900–1990*, ed. Charles Harrison and Paul Wood (Oxford, 1996), p. 148.

19 René Magritte, letter to Louis Quiévreux, 1967, in Blavier, ed., *René Magritte*, p. 253.

20 Magritte, 'Interview Quievreux' [1947], in Blavier, ed., *René Magritte*, p. 251.

21 Magritte, 'La Ligne de vie I', in *René Magritte*, ed. Blavier, pp. 108–9.

22 I am grateful to Marie Godet for pointing this out to me.

23 Haim Finkelstein, *The Screen in Surrealist Art and Thought* (Aldershot and Burlington, VT, 2007), p. 162.

24 René Magritte, letter to Paul Nougé, February 1930, in *CR III*, p. 349.

25 *Le Journal amusant*, IX/1 (21 February 1926), p. 15.

26 *CR I*, p. 198.

27 Magritte, 'La Psychanalyse' [1962], in *René Magritte*, ed. Blavier, pp. 558–9: p. 558.

28 David Sylvester, *Magritte* (London, 1992), p. 14.

29   *L'Indépendance Belge* (1 September 1907), p. 4.

30   *L'Indépendance Belge* (3 April 1909), p. 3.

31   *Gazette de Charleroi* (8 June 1913), p. 3.

32   Magritte, 'La Ligne de vie I', p. 106.

33   Duane Michals, *A Visit with Magritte* (Providence, RI, 1981).

34   René Magritte, letter to the Scutenaires, 17 December 1965, in *CR III*,
     p. 132.

Select Bibliography

Allain, Marcel, and Pierre Souvestre, *Fantômas* (London, 1986)

Allmer, Patricia, 'Framing the Real: Frames and the Processes of Framing in René Magritte's Oeuvre', in *Framing Borders in Literature and Other Media*, ed. Werner Wolf and Walter Bernhart (Amsterdam and New York, 2006), pp. 113–38

—, 'Dial "M" for Magritte', in *Johan Grimonprez: Looking for Alfred*, ed. Steven Bode and Thomas Elsaesser (London, 2007), pp. 208–23

—, *René Magritte: Beyond Painting* (Manchester, 2009)

Alquié, Ferdinand, *Entretiens sur le surréalisme*, ed. Ferdinand Alquié (Paris, 1968)

Blavier, André, ed., *René Magritte: Écrits Complets* (Paris, 2001)

Breton, André, *Manifestoes of Surrealism*, trans. Richard Seaver and Helen R. Lane (Ann Arbor, MI, 1972)

—, *Surrealism and Painting*, trans. Simon Watson Taylor (London, 1972)

Calvocoressi, Richard, *Magritte* (London, 1998)

Dell, Simon, 'Love and Surrealism: René Magritte and André Breton in 1929', *Word and Image*, XIX/3 (July–September 2003), p. 217

Dimbourg, Philippe, *La Foire autrefois en Wallonie et à Bruxelles* (Brussels, 2005)

Draguet, Michel, *Magritte* (Paris, 2014)

Durozoi, Gérard, *History of the Surrealist Movement* (London, 2002)

Elder, R. Bruce, *Dada, Surrealism, and the Cinematic Effect* (Waterloo, ON, 2015)

Éluard, Paul, 'René Magritte', *Cahiers d'art*, vols V–VI (1935), pp. 130–31

Ernst, Max, 'Beyond Painting', trans. D. Tanning, in *Beyond Painting*, ed. Robert Motherwell (New York, 1948), pp. 15–27.

Finkelstein, Haim, *The Screen in Surrealist Art and Thought* (Aldershot and Burlington, VT, 2007)

Grunenberg, Christoph, and Darren Pih, *Magritte A to Z* (Liverpool, 2011)

Handler Spitz, Ellen, *Museums of the Mind* (London, 1994)

Kunstverein und Kunsthaus Hamburg, *René Magritte und der Surrealismus in Belgien*, exh. cat., Kunstverein (Brussels, 1982)

Magritte, René, 'Leçon de choses: Ecrits et dessins de René Magritte', *Rhétorique*, 7 (October 1962), n.p.

Mercks, Jean-Louis, 'Ceux qui ne sont pas éternellement jeunes ont toujours été vieux', in *Hommage à Paul-Gustave Van Hecke*, ed. André De Rache (Brussels, 1969)

Michals, Duane, *A Visit with Magritte* (Providence, RI, 1981)

Miller Robinson, Fred, *The Man in the Bowler Hat: His History and Iconography* (Chapel Hill, NC, 1993)

Nead, Lynda, *The Haunted Gallery: Painting, Photography, Film, c. 1900* (New Haven, CT, 2007)

Nougé, Paul, *Histoire de ne pas rire* (Lausanne, 1980)

—, *Fragments* (Brussels, 1995)

Paquet, Marcel, *René Magritte, 1898–1967* (San Diego, CA, 1997)

Roegiers, Patrick, *Magritte and Photography* (London, 2005)

Rooney, Kathleen and Eric Plattner, eds, *René Magritte: Selected Writings*, trans. Jo Levy (Richmond, 2016)

Rosemont, Franklin, *What is Surrealism? Selected Writings* (London, 1978)

Rosenstock, Laura, 'De Chirico's Influence on the Surrealists', in *De Chirico*, ed. William Rubin, exh. cat., Museum of Modern Art (New York, 1982), pp. 111–30

Rothman, Roger, 'Against Sincerity: René Magritte, Paul Nougé and the Lesson of Paul Valéry', *Word and Image*, XXIII/3 (September 2007), pp. 305–14

Sylvester, David, *Magritte* (London, 1992)

—, and Sarah Whitfield, *René Magritte, Catalogue Raisonné*, vol. I: *Oil Paintings, 1916–1930* (Houston, TX, and London, 1992)

—, and Sarah Whitfield, *René Magritte, Catalogue Raisonné*, vol. II: *Oil Paintings and Objects, 1931–1948* (Antwerp, 1993)

—, and Sarah Whitfield, *Catalogue Raisonné*, vol. III: *Oil Paintings, Objects and Bronzes. 1949–1967* (London, 1993)

Thrall Soby, James, *René Magritte* (New York, 1965)

Torczyner, Harry, *Magritte: Zeichen und Bilder*, trans. Christiane Müller (Cologne, 1977)

Vovelle, José, *Le Surréalisme en Belgique* (Paris, 1972)

Waldberg, Patrick, *René Magritte*, trans. Austryn Wainhouse (Brussels, 1966)

Warner, Marina, *Phantasmagoria: Spirit Visions, Metaphors, and Media into the Twenty-first Century* (Oxford, 2006)

Whitfield, Sarah, *Magritte*, exh. cat., South Bank Centre (London, 1992)

Acknowledgements

My research has received long-term support from the René Magritte Estate and Duane Michals, and I am very grateful to both. Thanks are also due to Peter Colon at DC Moore Gallery, Gabe Fajuri and Potter & Potter Auctions, Inc., and to the Reaktion Books editorial and proofreading team for their careful attention to the text and images. In particular I want to thank my partner John Sears.

Earlier versions of the chapters were delivered as the Chaire Internationale Emile Bernheim lectures in May 2018.

Photo Acknowledgements